Tom Valenti's
SOUPS, STEWS, AND ONE-POT MEALS

125 Home Recipes from the Chef-Owner
of New York City's **Ouest** and 'Cesca

TOM VALENTI

AND

ANDREW FRIEDMAN

SCRIBNER

New York   London   Toronto   Sydney   Singapore

SCRIBNER
1230 Avenue of the Americas
New York, NY 10020

SCRIBNER and design are trademarks of
Macmillan Library Reference USA, Inc., used under license
by Simon & Schuster, the publisher of this work.

For information about special discounts for bulk purchases,
please contact Simon & Schuster Special Sales:
1-800-456-6798 or business@simonandschuster.com

Designed by Kyoko Watanabe
Text set in Stone Serif

Manufactured in the United States of America

1   3   5   7   9   10   8   6   4   2

Library of Congress Cataloging-in-Publication Data
Valenti, Tom, date.
[Soups, stews, and one-pot meals]
Tom Valenti's soups, stews, and one-pot meals : 125 home recipes from the chef-owner of New York City's
Ouest and 'Cesca / Tom Valenti and Andrew Friedman.
p. cm.
Includes index.
1. Soups. 2. Stews. 3. Casserole cookery. 4. Cookery, Italian. I. Friedman, Andrew, date. II. Title.
TX757.V35 2003
641.8'21—dc22
2003054479

ISBN 0-7432-4375-7

for Abigail,
T.V.

for Caitlin,
A.F.

This Book Does *Not* . . .

. . . call for hard-to-find ingredients;

. . . feature recipes within recipes;

. . . insist that you replicate complicated, origamilike presentations;

. . . assume that you can afford white truffles, caviar, or Kobe beef;

. . . ask you to eat sea urchin or blowfish;

. . . suggest vintage-specific wine pairings; or

. . . plug a line of bottled products.

Its mission is to share recipes for home meals that are simply prepared—most in a single vessel—and a chef's tips for making them as delicious as possible. That's it.

Contents

Tom Valenti's
SOUPS, STEWS, AND
ONE-POT MEALS

Foreword

Tom Valenti is a lot like me. We both hail from working-class Italian-American families. We both loved sports growing up (and still do). We both live happy lives cooking for the greatest customers in the world in New York City. We both love to fish and we both love to take naps. We both love to cook at our restaurants and at our homes. We both love big gutsy flavors and layers and layers of them in every dish we create. We both would prefer to be known for our grandma style of cooking than for anything "cutting-edge." We both represent the Italian ideal of hospitality and live for our love of the table and the time spent there with friends and family. We both understand the value of food as substance more than just something to eat. We both work with excellent charities outside of our restaurants and feel great about that.

. . . And we both hate doing the dishes.

This new book attacks the dishes issue head on. I find it deplorable that at the end of every great meal there is the equivalent of a prison sentence of an hour or more of cleanup for some unlucky soul. At our restaurants, we both have teams of people near us at all times to wipe up our every spill, to polish our fancy wine glasses, and to buff the silver. At home we have only ourselves.

The reality of cooking at home is not only that of the cleanup, it is also an issue of our most precious commodity: free time. Really great food does not have to take all day to prepare. Although they may need to simmer on the back burner for several hours on low heat, many of my favorite dishes take literally thirty minutes of real effort to get going. What that leaves is twofold: a great dish filled with exquisite and complex layers of poetic flavor and the ethereal texture of the best of grandma's cooking *and* the reality of a clean kitchen at dinnertime with but one pot and some plates to clean.

It's not that cleanup is such a crucial issue, because in fact I can always cajole someone into doing the dishes in exchange for dinner. It is more a matter of quality of life. The foods that come out of a single pot reflect the love of sharing and a time for family and the feelings of goodness that surround and envelop a table of people breaking bread in a near sacred hymn of ritual and simplicity. Conversely, it speaks to the modern family on the go, where dinners are often reheated three or four times a night, for each lone ship passing through the kitchen for just enough time to refuel. In this case a simmering pot of something great is a guarantee of higher quality food, even if quality time is less of a priority than it could be.

It may seem like slumming for one of New York City's greatest chefs to take on the Crock Pot, unless you really look at the menus in his instantly hot two restaurants, Ouest and 'Cesca. Deep behind the menu-speak describing the modern American and Italian ingredients in his timeless dishes, there lurks the real truth about Tom Valenti's cooking: each item is either cooked two minutes or two hours. The two-hour items are what make Tom's and my cooking so similar and so tasty, the two-minute items are what allow our restaurants to thrive. To understand that these two strategies can and should go together is critical in developing a strategy for cooking at home. Some things will take some time to cook into a potful of poetry. Other things take just a couple of minutes of prep to get ready. This is good. And there are some things, like a perfect plum or deliciously al dente spaghetti with oil and garlic, that are all about the shopping and not at all about the cook. In Tom's and my world, putting them all together makes for great food, and it should in yours.

So use this book with the same sense of humor and fun that Tom and I put into our daily adventures in cooking, buy the freshest ingredients you can find, use the recipes as road maps as opposed to exact surgical diagrams, and relax. There won't even be too much cleanup. Then you can eat just like Tom and I.

—*Mario Batali*

Introduction

Picture this: It's late in the evening. You're sitting in the living room, enjoying the company of family and friends, and savoring the final moments of a dinner party that began hours ago. Everything has been just perfect and everyone is so comfortable and sated that, if it were socially acceptable, they would close their eyes and nod off right there. Instead, they push themselves up out of their chairs, say goodnight, and retire to their cars or bedrooms.

You make your way around your home, turning off lights, closing windows. But then you reach the kitchen, and that warm, satisfied feeling deserts you as you're reminded of the monumental cleanup that awaits. Pots and pans have been turned every which way to fit into the sink; the last ones you used remain on the stovetop with remnants of meat and sauce encrusted—for eternity, or so it seems—onto their surfaces. Your heart sinks. Your elbow and wrist begin to ache at the mere contemplation of the task before you. Whether you tackle it tonight or leave it for the morning, one thing's for sure: It ain't gonna be fun.

To be perfectly honest, as much as anything else, this book began with my dread of that moment. Chefs probably hate washing dishes and scrubbing pots and pans more than anyone because there are people who do it for us in our restaurants. We live in a world where the supply of clean pots and pans is limitless and dirty ones simply don't exist. When we're done cooking, we're done working.

This is every bit as appealing as it sounds, and it gets even better: As you might know, we also have prep cooks who wash and pick the leaves from herbs, cut onions, make stocks, and so on. In other words, when I'm on the job, I can focus exclusively on the dish before me, drawing from prechopped and precooked ingredients.

When I cook at home, I try to approximate my work environment, whittling the cooking universe down to the burner in front of me, but never forgetting that I don't have a support staff to chop and clean. As a result, I depend almost exclusively on one-pot dishes where everything cooks together—often slowly, but sometimes quickly—in a single vessel. For the most part, one-pots call for a minimum of prep work, usually just chopping some vegetables and measuring the necessary quantities of broth, wine, vinegar, spices, and herbs. And there's only one pot to wash when I'm done.

▪ One Pot (Pretty Much): How It Works ▪

In the pages that follow, I'm going to show you how to make recipes as diverse and far-reaching as Butternut Squash Soup with Minced Bacon (page 37), Chicken in Red Wine Sauce (page 156), and Texas-Style Chili (page 114) in one cooking vessel. In the disclaimer department, you should know that my definition of one-pot cooking is any recipe that allows the principal cooking to take place in one vessel on the stovetop, in the oven, or both. I don't count mixing bowls, or even a pot or cookie sheet that might be used for a simple step like boiling pasta, blanching greens, or roasting vegetables. In a few cases, I actually use a second pot to accelerate the process, like steaming a large quantity of mussels in two pots simultaneously for Mussels with Tomato and Saffron (page 54).

The premise and promise of all one-pot cooking relies on the same basic logic: A steady building of flavors, one on top of the other, as opposed to what's known as "component cooking," where you must make a handful of different recipes to create the final dish.

In one-pot cooking, everything happens in one place, in that little space you've whittled your cooking universe down to. In some cases, browned meats may need to be temporarily removed and set aside; in others, a few of the ingredients may not be added until the final minutes of cooking. But in every instance, the technique itself really couldn't be simpler, calling for little more than periodic pouring, stirring and, best of all, tasting.

Much as I'd love to claim credit for it, one-pot cooking is obviously nothing new. Quite the opposite, in fact: Home cooks and chefs have been doing it for centuries. I'm endlessly amused by some of the ironies that abound around the history of this style of cooking. Think about how many classics we all still love today were born out of poverty generations ago. Dishes such as Beer and Beef Stew (page 116), Braised Oxtail with Cipolline Onions (page 180), and White Bean Casserole with Preserved Duck (page 108) are rich in flavor, and all descend from a similarly humble ancestry, based on recipes that were created as a way to break down and soften relatively tough (and therefore relatively cheap) cuts of meat.

I have a lot in common with many of these dishes. I'm descended from a humble but proud ancestry myself. I grew up in an Italian-American household where most of the cooking was done by my grandmother, a member of an entire generation of immigrant home cooks responsible for bringing Old World cooking to American kitchens. My grandmother wasn't a showoff, but her food was so intensely flavored, so primal and immediate, that she constantly impressed us nonetheless.

My grandmother didn't only cook one-pot dishes, but much of what she made was prepared that way, such as her tomato sauces (the flavor is a friendly ghost that haunts me to this day) and braised meats. She also taught me some great seafood recipes such as Tubetti with White Wine and Clams (page 92).

When I look back on my personal life and cooking career, I realize that one-pot dishes have always been there. They were there during my childhood. And they were there when, as a young professional cook, I traveled overseas to work for the acclaimed French chef Guy Savoy in his Paris restaurant. While in France—in bistros and in the homes of friends—I learned to appreciate the classic foods of that country. Many of them were made in one pot, such as Beef Bourguignon (page 120); Baked Chicken with Bacon, Mushrooms, and Pearl Onions (page 150); and *boeuf à la ficelle,* which inspired my Beef on a String Soup and Sandwich (page 176). In time, experimenting in my own home kitchen, I even found ways to cook a one-pot variation of those that weren't.

When I returned to New York, I worked at Gotham Bar and Grill as Alfred Portale's first sous chef. Alfred's food is very different from mine—he is a former jewelry designer, and his brilliantly conceived (and highly influential) dishes are visually unparalleled, usually drawing on several creations that are prepared separately. But we both grew up on Italian-American home cooking and had spent time in France, and I recognized some of that personal history even in his groundbreaking creations.

When I became the Executive Chef of Alison on Dominick Street, I began to let my love for my culinary roots show. And people responded like you wouldn't believe. I became famous for braised lamb shank. I'm still known for it. I've cooked at other New York City restaurants since then, including Cascabel, Butterfield 81, and the ones I now co-own, Ouest and 'Cesca. Over the years, I've forged a style of cooking that in many ways is based on my love of home cooking, featuring lots of soups, stews, braises, and roasts like the ones in this book. And customers respond more positively than ever, often telling me that they find my cooking comforting, largely because it's not the least bit intellectually challenging. Sometimes they say this sheepishly, as though they might be offending me, but I take it as the highest compliment.

Even beyond the kitchen, I think of myself as a one-pot kind of guy. I believe that when you can keep things simple without sacrificing quality, you should. That's part of why I love to cook and eat things like the woodsy, rustic Mushroom, Barley, and Sage Soup (page 32); the beefaroni-meets-béchamel Lamb Pasticcio (page 124); and the timeless Baked Chicken with Bacon, Mushrooms, and Pearl Onions (page 150). I actually appreciate them more, and think they taste a little better, because they're so refreshingly easy to make.

Speaking of keeping things simple, of taking a one-pot view of the world, here's my goal as we move forward together: I want this book to inspire you to run into the kitchen and find out for yourself how doable these and other bursting-with-flavor dishes are.

▪ In Praise of Slow Cooking ▪

Many of the recipes in this book are cooked slowly over a period of several hours. As far as I'm concerned, *slow* is one of the most evocative words in a food-lover's vocabulary; the mere mention of slow cooking starts my mouth watering. When we speak of slow cooking, we speak of home cooking. We speak of lovingly prepared dishes that require a minimum of effort yet produce sensuous textures; deep, abiding flavors; and soul-nourishing satisfaction. It brings to mind succulent roasted leg of lamb, home-style tomato sauces, a spicy chili, or a savory pot roast. It reminds us that our sense of smell accounts for ninety percent of our sense of taste—you can really *taste* these dishes just by taking in their potent aromas.

My favorite food memories are based on slow cooking, like when I think back on my grandmother standing over a pot, wooden spoon in hand, or when I remember walking into her house and being embraced by kitchen scents that seemed as loving and welcoming as a hug from the woman herself. No matter what your background or biography, I bet that slow cooking reminds you of home, or of what you think home should be.

In today's fast-paced world, it's nice to be known for something so humble. At my restaurant Ouest the menu overflows with other slow-cooked offerings, including Mushroom-Braised Short Ribs (page 174) and Red-Wine-and-Tomato-Braised Duck (page 106). And that's nothing compared to my at-home repertoire, which includes such personal favorites as Chicken Braised with Mushrooms (page 154); Root Vegetable Stew with Cumin, Coriander, and Millet (page 78); and Braised Pork Belly in White Wine Sauce (page 192).

Ironically, slow cooking is the perfect answer to the scheduling challenges facing today's fast-forwarding, double-clicking, express-lane-shopping home cooks. These are recipes that may take their sweet time getting where they're going, but they don't insist that you come along for the ride. Slow-cooked meals are their own, self-reliant workhorses. You get them started, and off they go—or rather off you go, leaving them to their own exquisite transformations. While you're away, meat softens to fork-tenderness (a state of culinary nirvana where it flakes or breaks apart at the touch or tug of a fork), dense root vegetables develop the ability to melt in your mouth, and braising liquids amass mind-blowing layers of flavor. All you really need to do once you've got such a dish under way is check on it every now and then, maybe rotate something a turn every half hour or so, and then just dig in and enjoy—or sometimes, even better, set aside to enjoy the next day when you can sit down to a satisfying, ready-made meal.

Equal Time (Actually, Less Time): In Praise of Fast Cooking

There are also a number of one-pot recipes in this book that cook quickly, most of them featuring fish or shellfish. But I hasten to add that dishes like Sautéed Calamari with White Wine, Garlic, and Clam Broth (page 100); Roasted Fish and Shellfish with Tomatoes and Parsley (page 98); and Baked Sea Bass, Papillote Style, with Lemon and Olives (page 146) don't offer less flavor than other recipes in this book. It simply means that fish and shellfish, as a rule, take relatively little time to cook. The overall character of these dishes may be somewhat lighter than that of their poultry and meat counterparts, but they still feature my trademark flourishes, like the unmistakable acidic lift of distilled white vinegar and the smoky undercurrent of bacon and other pork products. And everything is still mingling in one vessel, building in flavor and complexity by the minute.

Make-Ahead Cooking That Gets Better Every Day

I'm a big believer in make-ahead cooking and many of the recipes in this book can be prepared in advance. Moreover, most of them get better over a day or two in the refrigerator for the same reason that cooking in one pot produces delicious results to begin with: The give and take of flavors—the way the ingredients enhance one another—is only reinforced the longer the ingredients intermingle.

To maximize this benefit, I've also provided suggestions for how to find inspiration with leftovers in a recurring feature called "Tomorrow's Table" that tells how to use them as a basis for a new dish. For example, turning Florentine Pot Roast with Red Wine, Mushrooms, and Tomatoes (page 178) into a pasta sauce by shredding the meat and heating it in the braising liquid, or making Lentil and Garlic Sausage Stew (page 110) into a soup with the addition of extra stock and fresh herbs. These uses expand on the economy and efficiency of the recipes.

▪ Throw It Right In ▪

One of the pleasant surprises I discovered while testing recipes for this book is that a great many ingredients that most recipes instruct you to precook on their own can be added in their dried form and successfully reconstituted right in the pot where you're making the main dish. Barley, millet, dried porcini mushrooms, and a bunch of other ingredients all cook perfectly well in this way.

Not only does this save time, but it also makes more of an impact on the dish. Mushrooms, for instance, have more time to infuse the liquid with their flavor. Note these skip-a-step tips in the recipes for your own spontaneous cooking. They'll make both cooking and cleaning faster.

▪ Save Another Step: Cook It and Serve It, in the Same Pot ▪

Many of the dishes in this book can be served right from their cooking vessel, plunked down in the center of the table. Be careful to protect your table. I suggest doing this in a way that emphasizes the recipes' rustic roots. Place a wooden cutting board on the table (the older and more dramatic-looking, the better), lay a cloth napkin on it, and place the hot pot on top for a little display—a timeless touch that makes the meal all the more appealing.

How to Use This Book

▪ Cooking in the Real World ▪

If you own a number of chef books, then you're probably used to guys and gals in my line of work assuming that you make your own stocks, take the time to soak dried beans, and possess the deft hands required to imitate plating techniques that take professionals years to master.

This book is a little different. This book assumes that you live in a place that I like to call the Real World. In the Real World, you might have some homemade stock in the freezer, but it's more likely that you'll buy broth in a can or carton at the supermarket. In the Real World, it's possible that you'll think far ahead enough to soak beans overnight, but the likelihood is that you'll buy canned, cooked beans, like I do at home. In the Real World, you might very well be able to perch a piece of fish or chicken atop a pyramid of potatoes, and then get that little culinary seesaw to the table without it toppling, but I'm guessing that even if you could, you'd rather not bother.

Here are my recommendations for cooking in the Real World:

Cookware

What do you need for one-pot cooking? Just one pot, right? Well, actually, you might want just a few more pieces than that. Before I tell you what they are, a word about quality.

The old adage "you get what you pay for" really reverberates when it comes to cookware. A lot of home cooks experience sticker shock when they decide to upgrade to first-class equipment or buy a high-quality knife for the first time. But if you want to cook well, there's really no way around this. Just as you can't make great food with mediocre ingredients, you can't pull it off with inferior cookware. If you don't have good cookware, you'll never be able to truly control the interaction between food and heat. If that doesn't convince you, consider this: High-quality cookware lasts longer—in fact, if you treat it right, it'll last you a lifetime.

So get out there and treat yourself to some good pots. Materials vary; I prefer stainless steel for its look and durability and because it won't impart any flavor to the food the way, say, aluminum will. At the top of the cookware food chain is copper, which conducts heat better than any of its kin, and looks beautiful, but is far more expensive and a real hassle to keep clean and polished. If you end up splurging for copper, I recommend looking for pots lined with stainless steel, which unlike traditional tin linings will never need to be replaced.

Whatever material you choose, make sure your pots have metal handles so that they can go from the stovetop to the oven without hesitation.

What exactly should you buy? Well, in most of the recipes in this book, I refer to the cooking vessel as a "pot," by which I mean any large vessel. Most of the time, any of the following would work well:

- A 5-quart pot.
- A 2-gallon Dutch oven (a large pot with handles on both sides and a domed lid).
- An ovenproof casserole, any of a variety of cooking vessels that come in many shapes and sizes and are usually designed to be brought to the table. For the recipes in this book that specifically call for a casserole, such as Andrew and Caitlin's Soppressata Lasagna (page 126), a 3-quart capacity would be ideal. You have a choice here between cast iron, porcelain, earthenware, and enameled cast iron. I prefer the enameled variety because they're more resistant to wear and tear and because they're more attractive on the table.

- A roasting pan. You'll want this for those times when you simply need a lot of surface area to keep the ingredients from crowding. I usually call for this when braising several large pieces of meat like lamb shanks or short ribs.

If you want to round out your cookware collection, there are just a few more pieces I recommend:

- A stockpot. Go for one with a 2½-gallon capacity. In addition to being useful for making stock, it's great for cooking pasta and making large quantities of soup.
- An ovenproof glass baking dish. You can purchase these in a variety of sizes and shapes. They're relatively inexpensive, so I keep a small fleet on standby. If you only want one, I suggest you buy a 9-inch square dish that's 2 inches deep, which accommodates most pasta casseroles well and is a good size for serving at the table.
- A sauté pan. Make it big in all respects, with a lid that fits. I suggest a 12-inch stainless-steel pan with deep sides. You might not always need all that room, but when you do, you'll be glad you have it. For example, if you're making a pasta sauce, you can add the pasta directly to the pan and toss it there.
- A baking sheet. You'll want one of these for roasting vegetables and spreading hot ingredients out to cool. Buy one with a rim. As with that big sauté pan, you might not always need one, but you'll be glad to have it when you do. Be sure the pan you buy fits into your oven; 12 by 16 inches is usually a good bet.

Beyond cooking vessels, the equipment for cooking the recipes in this book is limited. You might want (but do not need) a good, long set of tongs for turning meats and fishing bay leaves out of soups, stews, and cooking liquids; a long wooden spoon; a whisk; and a ladle.

Finally, there's no more important implement before you start cooking than a good, sharp, stainless-steel knife with a single, forged blade. Look for one whose handle is built around, or from, the back of the steel itself, which is the sturdiest, most unlikely to break, and will give you the best control of the blade. If you want to invest in only one, I say make it an 8-inch chef's knife, which you can use for everything from smashing garlic to carving large cuts of meat.

Stocks

The recipes in this book are so jam-packed with flavor that you can use store-bought stock or broth. I recommend you identify a brand that you like—one available at your local market—so that you're familiar with it and how it tastes. There's a wealth of important information on the label or carton. For flavor's sake, the most important consideration is that it is low in sodium so you can control the salt in the dish. In extreme cases, an excess of sodium can ruin things right off the bat. If your options are limited and you can only put your hands on high-sodium broth, dilute it by one-third with water. I also encourage you to veer toward stocks that have as many appealing adjectives as possible, like "all-natural," and "organic." A lot of commercial stocks also contain MSG (monosodium glutamate), which is a whole other can of worms. Avoid these if possible.

All of that said, if you make your own stocks at home on a regular basis, you're a better person than I and you should by all means use them. (To nudge you in this direction, I've included recipes for some basic stocks in the appendix.) In the few cases where they might make a huge difference in flavor, like Spinach, Parmesan, and Garlic Soup (page 34), I'll let you know.

Because of the great discrepancies that occur from broth to broth and stock to stock, I'm not precise in the measurements I give for salt and pepper in the soup recipes, where the liquid itself plays such a central role. However, in many of the recipes for braises and roasts, where the stock isn't as predominant, I give specific quantities for seasoning.

Beans and Legumes

I've got a pretty spontaneous appetite, so it's rare that I plan a home meal a day in advance. Consequently, I don't really have time to soak beans. I also don't see the need. There are so many top-notch canned, cooked beans available that it just doesn't seem necessary to me. As with those broths, find a good, reliable brand (I love Goya) and be sure to drain and rinse them before adding them to the pot; this will keep their starchy liquid from clouding up the dish and altering the flavor of the soup.

Variations

Here you'll find suggestions for ways to create something a little different by altering the recipe at hand, for example turning Spinach, Parmesan, and Garlic Soup (page 34) into the sauce for gnocchi (page 88); Manhattan-Style Fish Stew (page 96) into Mediterranean Fish Stew with olives and capers; and Macaroni and Goat Cheese (page 90) into a Two-Cheese Macaroni featuring mozzarella and Parmesan and topped with chopped basil.

Tomorrow's Table

This is where I offer suggestions for how to use leftovers creatively, like turning the Butternut Squash and Wild Mushroom Risotto (page 82) into fried risotto cakes or making Mushroom-Braised Short Ribs (page 174) into a killer sandwich. Despite all this advice, it should be noted that in almost every case the original dish will also be even better the second day without embellishment, so simply enjoying it again is always an option.

At the end of the book, you'll find two appendices called "Accompaniments and Additions" and "Condiments and Garnishes." Both are full of recipes that will help you add even more appealing flavors and textures to the pot with little extra work. You'll also find "Notes on Recurring Ingredients" which offers some insight into why I use certain ingredients such as bacon and distilled white vinegar so damn much, as well as tips for some basic kitchen procedures, including peeling tomatoes. My hope is that you'll find this information useful in successfully following recipes, both from this book and elsewhere.

I think you'll be surprised by how much you can accomplish in a single pot, from soups to pastas to casseroles to braises to roasts . . . to that all-so-easy cleanup at the end of the meal. So, let's go. The sooner we get started, the sooner we eat.

Hearty Soups
and Chowders

I've noticed something about soup in every restaurant in which I've cooked over the years: Customers absolutely love it. Not just a particular soup—though everyone has his or her favorite—but soup as a category. As I've been cooking professionally for more than twenty years, I have to conclude that this is more than a passing fancy.

I attribute soup's perennial popularity to the fact that even in today's wildly experimental restaurants where there's always a newly discovered ingredient just around the corner, soups exude a warm, homey aura. When a bowl of soup is placed in front of my customers, you can see the stress of the day lift from their shoulders as they settle a little more comfortably in their seats.

I, too, have a fondness for soups, even more as a home cook than as a restaurant chef, or even a restaurant-goer.

Among soup's most enticing attributes in the home kitchen is that virtually all of them can be made ahead of time and refrigerated for a few days or frozen for a month or more. Rare is the soup that doesn't lend itself to advance preparation: Cream soups can be made ahead, if you don't add the cream until after thawing and reheating, and even seafood soups, like chowders, can be revived after a period of suspended animation. (As user-friendly as soups are in this regard, there is one important tip to bear in mind: If you choose to make soups ahead and freeze them, stop the cooking a few minutes early, leaving the vegetables and other key ingredients a bit al dente; this will keep them from breaking down when thawed and reheated.)

Something else I just adore about soups is that even the simplest of them can be elevated into something special with the addition of fresh herbs, a drizzle of excellent extra-virgin or infused olive oil, or a dusting of grated Parmesan or Pecorino Romano cheese. Accompaniments such as a crouton spread with Aïoli (garlic mayonnaise, page 230) or topped with melted cheese, can also make soup into more of an event.

Personally, I'm partial to soups that—as that commercial says—eat like a meal. Along these lines, soup can be turned into a bona fide main event with the addition of a generous dose of rice, couscous, millet, or other grains. (See page 207 for more on this.) Pasta achieves the same end, but stay away from those that are excessively starchy, including pappardelle or other large-cut fresh pasta, for two reasons: (a) A certain amount of their starch ends up in the cooking liquid, which can cloud the soup, and (b) They can soak up more of the soup than you'd like, so you end up serving people bowls of bloated noodles. Small, dried pasta like pastina or orzo (page 217) are the way to go here.

A number of the "Variations" and "Tomorrow's Table" tips in this chapter outline specific ways to embellish a soup by adding vegetables or meats, or to extend a soup by simply adding more stock. But don't limit yourself to my suggestions. Adaptability is an inherent quality of almost every soup on earth. Think about all of those famous soups of Italy and France such as Pasta and Bean Soup (page 24); Tomato, Bread, and Parmesan Soup (page 40); Twice-Cooked Vegetable Soup (page 46); and Lobster Bisque (page 57) that differ from kitchen to kitchen, but are always recognizable nonetheless. I encourage you to follow that spirit yourself, experimenting with soups by altering them according to your own taste.

Soup's Magic Wand

Without a doubt, the most useful soup-making tool to arrive on the market in recent years is the immersion blender, which goes by a number of names, such as hand blender or blending wand. You've probably seen this lovely little gadget: It's a handheld stick with a little dome on the end that covers a blending blade. Its first incarnation was as a professional kitchen tool, but affordable home models are readily available today and I urge you to buy one as soon as possible.

When it comes to soups, the usefulness of the immersion blender cannot be overstated. If making a pureed soup, you can puree the ingredients right in the pot, eliminating the need to transfer them to a blender or food processor. No more working in batches! Or, if you want to puree just a portion of the solids to thicken a soup—such as Potato and Leek Soup (page 44) or Ham Hock and Split Pea Soup (page 66)—give it a few zaps with an immersion blender and you're all set.

There's something else I love about this gadget: I have an intense fear of litigation, and immersion blenders assuage my anxiety over home cooks putting hot liquids in a blender or food processor, which can be dangerous for even professional cooks. Heat can force the lid right off, spraying extremely hot soup all over you (and your walls).

As with all rules, this one has its exceptions. Some soups, such as Butternut Squash Soup with Minced Bacon (page 37) and Roasted Carrot and Ginger Soup (page 27) benefit from being pureed in a blender or food processor, where the circulation of the liquid and solids helps integrate the flavors better. Don't worry; I'll let you know when this is the case. When using a food processor or blender, don't fill the bowl more than one-third of the way to the top, and remove the lid's central piece to allow steam to escape. For extra measure, cover the lid with a towel to keep any hot liquid from escaping.

Pasta and Bean Soup

■ *Serves 8* ■

Next to its celebration of creamy white beans, my favorite thing about this soup is the way its name is pronounced by Italian-Americans: "pasta fazool," simply a fast and fun way of saying *pasta e fagioli*. Typical of many Italian dishes, the recipe for this soup varies from home to home. You might see it made with different beans, fresh pasta instead of dried, and with heartier stocks.

The consistency of the soup is a matter of personal preference. A lot of American chefs puree this soup to thicken it, but my first taste of *pasta e fagioli* was in my grandmother's kitchen, where soups were *never* pureed. Taking her lead, I thicken the soup by mashing a potato that's been cooked in the broth itself and stirring it back into the liquid, leaving each and every bean intact and ready to be savored in all its natural glory.

Like most of the recipes in this chapter, this one can be made in advance, but don't add the pasta until the soup has been reheated or the noodles will expand like sponges and turn this into a watery pasta dish. For the same reason, if you only serve a portion of the soup at a time, keep the amount you don't use separate and pasta-free.

Serve this with Herbed or Cheese Croutons (pages 232 and 233), if desired.

2 tablespoons olive oil
¼ pound prosciutto di Parma, cut into medium dice (double-smoked bacon can be substituted, see page 241)
1 small carrot, peeled and cut into small dice
1 small Spanish onion, peeled and cut into small dice
1 stalk celery, cut into small dice
2 cloves garlic, smashed and peeled
Coarse salt

Freshly ground black pepper
1 heaping tablespoon tomato paste
1 quart store-bought, reduced-sodium vegetable broth or homemade Vegetable Stock (page 244)
1 quart water
2 medium baking potatoes, peeled
One 1-pound-13-ounce can cannellini beans, rinsed and drained
1 cup dried ditalini pasta, cooked and drained (page 217)

1 tablespoon chopped fresh	¼ cup freshly grated Parmesan cheese,
rosemary	plus more for sprinkling
Pinch of crushed red pepper	Extra-virgin olive oil

1. Heat the olive oil in a large, heavy-bottomed pot over medium heat. Add the prosciutto and cook, stirring, until the prosciutto begins to render its fat, about 5 minutes.

2. Add the carrot, onion, celery, and garlic. Season with salt and pepper and cook, stirring, until softened but not browned, about 5 minutes. Add the tomato paste, stir to coat the other ingredients, and cook for 2 minutes. Add the broth, water, and potatoes. Raise the heat to high and bring to a boil, then lower the heat and simmer until the potatoes are very soft (a sharp, thin-bladed knife should easily pierce their center), about 20 minutes. Use tongs or a slotted spoon to transfer the potatoes to a bowl. Mash the potatoes with a masher or a large fork or spoon.

3. Return the mashed potatoes to the pot and stir them into the soup. If not serving immediately, let cool, cover and refrigerate for a few days or freeze for up to 1 month. Reheat before proceeding.

4. Add the beans and pasta. Cook over medium heat until the beans are warmed through, about 5 minutes. Stir in the rosemary, crushed red pepper, and cheese. Taste and adjust the seasoning with salt and pepper, if necessary.

5. To serve, ladle some soup into each of 8 bowls. Top with some more cheese and a drizzle of extra-virgin olive oil.

VARIATIONS

Chickpea Soup

For a soup that's less Italian in character, and more generally Mediterranean, omit the pasta, replace the cannellini beans with an equal quantity of chickpeas, and increase the cooking time by 5 to 10 minutes, until the chickpeas are tender and warmed through.

Cassoulet Soup

If you love cassoulet, the highly adaptable French bean stew that can include everything from sausage to duck to poultry, you can use this recipe to do a pretty good impression of one: Omit the pasta and add 3 or 4 (4-ounce) links sweet Italian sausage that have been cut into ½-inch rounds and browned, or use coarsely chopped, store-bought duck confit (see Mail-Order Sources, page 247).

Roasted Carrot and Ginger Soup

■ Serves 8 ■

Sweet carrot and peppery ginger are a can't-miss marriage that's enhanced here by roasting the carrots before making the soup. Because carrots and ginger are so inexpensive, and there are few other ingredients to buy, this recipe promises one of the most impressive cost-to-taste ratios of all time. If you want to make it even easier, don't roast the carrots; simply cut the raw, peeled carrots into small dice, omit Steps one and two, and add them to the pot along with the ginger and bay leaf in Step four. If you do this, increase the cooking time to forty-five minutes.

A blender will give you the silkiest possible soup here, but you could also use an immersion blender or food processor.

2 pounds carrots (about 4 large carrots), peeled and trimmed
¼ cup olive oil
Coarse salt
Freshly ground black pepper
Sugar, if needed
1 medium Spanish onion, peeled and cut into small dice
1 stalk celery, cut into small dice

2 tablespoons grated fresh ginger
1 bay leaf
1½ quarts store-bought, reduced-sodium vegetable broth or homemade Vegetable Stock (page 244)
1 tablespoon unsalted butter
Fried Shallots (page 235), optional

1. Preheat the oven to 325°F.

2. Rub the carrots with 2 tablespoons of the olive oil and place on a rimmed baking sheet in a single layer. Sprinkle with salt and pepper, rotating the carrots to season all over. If the carrots seem dry or lack a bright orange color, season with a few pinches of sugar as well. Place the sheet in the oven and roast the carrots, shaking the sheet occasionally to turn them, until quite tender, about 1 hour. (Test for doneness by piercing the carrots with a sharp, thin-bladed knife; they're done when it pierces right through to their center.) Remove the baking sheet from the oven and let the car-

rots cool slightly. Trim and discard any overcaramelized bits and cut the carrots into 1-inch segments.

3. Heat the remaining 2 tablespoons olive oil in a large, heavy-bottomed pot over medium-high heat until hot but not yet smoking. Add the onion and celery, season with salt and pepper, and cook until softened but not browned, about 5 minutes.

4. Add the carrots, ginger, and bay leaf and cook, stirring, for 1 minute. Add the broth, bring the liquid to a boil, then lower the heat, partially cover, and simmer until the carrots begin to break apart when prodded with a spoon, about 30 minutes.

5. Use tongs or a slotted spoon to fish out and discard the bay leaf. Transfer the contents of the pot to a blender, add the butter, and process for several minutes, until uniformly smooth and creamy. You may need to do this in batches (see safety tip, page 23). If not serving immediately, let cool, cover, and refrigerate for a few days or freeze for up to 1 month.

6. Return the soup to the pot and reheat gently. Taste and correct the seasoning with salt, pepper, and sugar, if necessary. (Don't be shy with the sugar, this soup should be unabashedly sweet.)

7. To serve, ladle some soup into each of 8 bowls and garnish with fried shallots, if desired.

VARIATIONS

Roasted Carrot, Ginger, and Shellfish Soup

For a soup that could be enjoyed as a light meal, poach 2 pounds of shelled, deveined shrimp in simmering water until firm and pink, 3 to 5 minutes, or cook and remove the meat from three 1-pound lobsters (see page 57 for instructions), and cut it into ½-inch pieces. Divide the shellfish among the bowls before ladling the soup over it. Feel free to cook and cool the shellfish in advance; the hot soup will reheat the meat. Alternatively, you can place 2 ounces of cleaned, fresh crabmeat in each bowl.

Roasted Parsnip and Ginger Soup

If you love parsnips, use them here. Simply replace the carrots with an equal quantity of parsnips. Look for smaller parsnips, which have less tuberous fiber in the center and puree more easily. Depending on their size, parsnips roast more quickly than carrots; check them after 40 minutes. For a slightly sweeter soup, use 1 pound each of carrots and parsnips.

Silken Corn Puree

■ *Serves 8* ■

Maybe I'm just a cynic, but I hate when people describe food as a season on a plate or in a bowl. Expressions like "You won't believe this fresh-cut-grass salad, it's like spring on a plate," make me want to pull out what's left of my hair. But, I have to tell you, this soup *is* like summer in a bowl. I hate myself for saying it, but it's true.

I only make this soup in the summer when corn is at its annual peak of perfection, and I serve it hot because that's the only way to really taste all of the corn's flavor. Because it depends so thoroughly on the vegetable itself, only make this with super-fresh cobs.

The other thing I just adore about this is that it can be dressed to the nines with as many garnishes as you desire (see the note at the end of the recipe).

15 large ears corn, husked	Freshly ground black pepper
1 quart plus 1 cup whole milk	Sugar
Coarse salt	1 to 2 tablespoons unsalted butter

1. Cut the kernels off the cobs by standing each cob on end and slicing downward with a large, sharp chef's knife, rotating the cob until all the kernels are removed. You should have 6 to 7 cups of kernels. Then repeat this action against the cob itself, this time running the blunt back edge of the knife down the cob to draw out any remaining moisture.

2. Transfer the kernels and their liquid to the bowl of a food processor and add just enough of the milk for the blade to start moving. Puree the corn until thick and smooth.

3. Transfer the pureed corn to a large, heavy-bottomed pot and set over medium heat. Bring to a simmer and cook, whisking constantly, until it warms and thickens, about 15 minutes. Season with salt, pepper, and a pinch of sugar. Gradually whisk the remaining milk into the soup.

4. Pour the soup through a fine-mesh strainer, pushing down on the solids with a rubber spatula to extract as much liquid as possible. Discard the solids. Whisk the butter into the soup to enrich it. If not serving immediately, let cool, cover, and refrigerate for a few days or freeze for up to 1 month.

5. Return the liquid to the pot and reheat gently. Taste and adjust the seasoning if necessary. Ladle the soup into 8 individual bowls. Garnish to your heart's content and serve at once.

VARIATIONS

Creamed Corn
For delicious creamed corn, simply stop after Step 3.

Chunky Corn Soup
Set one-third of the corn kernels aside before pureeing in Step 2, and return them to the pot just before serving.

GARNISHES

This recipe is a garnisher's paradise. For a chowderesque dish, stir in 1 pound cooked and shelled crab or lobster meat, or a cup of diced, boiled potato just before serving. You can also scatter minced, crisp bacon, chopped scallion, or crème fraîche and caviar over the top.

Mushroom, Barley, and Sage Soup

■ *Serves 8* ■

The simple addition of dried porcini and fresh sage to a fairly conservative recipe for mushroom and barley soup pays big dividends, adding a dark, woodsy depth of flavor that just might make this the best one you've ever tasted. Most versions simply add mushrooms and barley to a chicken or beef broth, but here the porcini infuse the entire soup with potent mushroom flavor. And stirring a generous quantity of sage in just before serving adds an earthy aroma that will have people appreciating the soup before the first spoonful reaches their lips.

If you want to go to the trouble and expense of buying wild mushrooms, such as chanterelles or oyster mushrooms, and roasting them (see the note at the end of the recipe), that's another way to add even more intense flavor.

2 tablespoons olive oil

1 large carrot, peeled and cut into small dice

1 medium Spanish onion, peeled and cut into small dice

1 stalk celery, cut into small dice

Coarse salt

Freshly ground black pepper

1½ pounds white mushrooms, brushed clean, stems discarded, thinly sliced

2 quarts store-bought, reduced-sodium beef broth

¾ cup pearl barley (page 207)

¼ cup dried porcini mushrooms (page 243), rinsed and crumbled by hand

2 tablespoons chopped fresh sage leaves

Garlic Croutons (page 233), optional

1. Heat the olive oil in a large, heavy-bottomed pot over medium-high heat until hot but not smoking. Add the carrot, onion, and celery, season with salt and pepper, and cook, stirring, until the vegetables are lightly browned, about 7 minutes. Add the white mushrooms, season with salt and pepper, and cook until they begin to give off their liquid, 5 to 7 minutes.

2. Add the broth and barley to the pot and bring the liquid to a boil over high heat.

Reduce the heat and simmer, covered, for 20 minutes. Add the porcini and simmer, still covered, until the barley is softened, but still a bit al dente, about 25 minutes longer, checking periodically to be sure the soup is simmering very gently so as not to break up the other ingredients. If not serving immediately, let cool, cover, and refrigerate for a few days or freeze for up to 1 month. Reheat before proceeding.

3. Stir in the sage. Taste and adjust the seasoning if necessary. Ladle into individual bowls and serve, garnishing with garlic croutons if desired.

VARIATIONS

Mushroom, Barley, and Short Rib Soup

If you have leftover Mushroom-Braised Short Ribs (page 174), remove the meat from the bones, cut the meat into small chunks, and toss it into the soup.

ROASTING MUSHROOMS

To roast wild mushrooms, preheat the oven to 350°F. For 1 pound mushrooms, pour ¾ cup olive oil into a small bowl. Add a smashed, peeled garlic clove and a few thyme sprigs; season with salt and pepper. Trim the stems and dip the mushrooms in the oil, letting any excess oil run off. Place the mushrooms on a rimmed baking sheet and roast in the oven until the mushrooms turn golden brown and begin to crisp around the edges, 15 to 18 minutes. If adding these mushrooms to a soup or stew (rather than serving them on their own), you can cool, cover, and refrigerate them for up to 24 hours. If using in the soup above, add them in Step 2 with the broth and barley.

Spinach, Parmesan, and Garlic Soup

■ *Serves 8* ■

This remarkably easy soup is based on one of those Italian dishes I grew up on. I can still remember my grandmother heating up some chicken broth, throwing in a handful of chopped spinach (she rarely used measuring cups or written recipes), and topping it with grated Parmesan at the table. This recipe is almost as elementary, and goes from pot to bowl in record time. It features just three primary components, but the trio is so well balanced—the green flavor of spinach, the bite of garlic, and the salty cheese—that it registers as satisfying and complete on the palate.

You can also make this soup with other greens like escarole (more bitter than spinach) and kale (more toothsome than spinach), just be sure to increase the cooking time by 4 or 5 minutes, depending on how tender you want them.

Because the stock itself plays such a major role here, this is one case where your homemade stock would be put to good use. You can also reinforce the cheesy flavor by serving Cheese Croutons (page 233) on the side, or the garlic flavor by topping each serving with a few Garlic Croutons (page 233).

2 tablespoons olive oil
1 small Spanish onion, peeled and
 minced
3 cloves garlic, peeled and minced
Coarse salt
Freshly ground black pepper
2 pounds spinach (about 3 large
 bunches), stems discarded, roughly
 chopped, rinsed, and left a little damp

2 quarts homemade Chicken Stock
 (page 244) or store-bought,
 reduced-sodium chicken broth
¼ cup freshly grated Parmesan
 cheese, plus more for serving
Extra-virgin olive oil, optional

1. Heat the olive oil in a large, heavy-bottomed pot over medium-high heat until hot but not smoking. Add the onion and garlic, season with salt and pepper, and cook, stirring, until softened but not browned, about 5 minutes.

2. Add the spinach to the pot and season with salt and pepper. The spinach will kick and spit a bit, which is what you want. Stir it with a kitchen spoon or tongs so that the spinach soaks up the flavor of the garlic and onion. Cook until all of the spinach takes on a bright green color, about 2 minutes.

3. Add the stock and stir. Bring it to a boil, then lower the heat and let the soup simmer for 5 minutes. If not serving immediately, let cool, cover, and refrigerate for a few days or freeze for up to 1 month. Reheat before proceeding.

4. Stir in the ¼ cup cheese and ladle some soup into each of 8 bowls. Top with a sprinkling of black pepper, a drizzle of extra-virgin olive oil if desired, and serve, passing extra grated cheese in a small bowl at the table.

VARIATIONS

Creamy Spinach, Parmesan, and Garlic Soup

To make a thicker, richer soup dominated by cheese, don't add the Parmesan in Step 4. Instead, strain the soup through a fine-mesh strainer, reserve the spinach, and blend the cheese into the broth using an immersion blender or regular blender (see safety tips, pages 22 and 23). Return the broth and reserved spinach to the pot to rewarm. You can also break an egg into a bowl, beat it, and stir it into the soup, off the heat, just before serving. Alternatively, you might top each serving with a poached egg and let each diner break it open and stir it in.

Spinach and White Bean Soup

Drain and rinse one 15-ounce can of cannellini beans and add them in Step 4 to heat though in the hot broth.

Spinach and Chicken Soup

Stir chopped leftover chicken, perhaps from the recipes on page 154, 158, or 160, into the soup for a more substantial dish.

Gnocchi with Spinach, Parmesan, and Garlic

Use the soup to flavor cooked gnocchi (page 88): Put the gnocchi in a deep-sided, heavy-bottomed sauté pan, pour 2 cups of the soup on top, and warm over moderate heat, stirring or tossing, for 3 to 5 minutes, then divide among individual plates. Top with extra grated Parmesan.

Butternut Squash Soup with Minced Bacon

■ *Serves 8* ■

Most recipes for butternut squash soup cook the squash right in the pot with the liquid. I find that the easy, extra step of roasting the squash beforehand removes more moisture, concentrating the vegetable's sweet autumn flavor. It also infuses the soup with smokiness thanks to the bacon that's laid atop the squash. (If you simply can't resist eating the bacon, feel free to snack on one of the pieces after it comes out of the oven. You'll still have enough to garnish the soup.) Stirring in cream or butter at the end is optional, but it makes a big difference, enriching the soup and pulling all of the ingredients together as smoothly as possible.

Because this soup is basically a squash puree thinned with broth, it's a good recipe to try with other squashes available at the market. Acorn works well, as does Hubbard, which is often overlooked for roasting and soups.

You can replace the minced bacon with a topping of Frizzled Leeks (page 236); either omit the bacon entirely, or roast the squash with the bacon, then devour the bacon as you make the soup.

6 pounds butternut squash
6 tablespoons unsalted butter
Coarse salt
Freshly ground black pepper
8 slices double-smoked bacon
    (page 241)
2 tablespoons olive oil
1 large Spanish onion, peeled and cut
    into small dice
3 thyme sprigs, plus extra leaves for
    serving

1 bay leaf
1½ quarts store-bought, reduced-
    sodium chicken broth or
    homemade Chicken Stock
    (page 244)
2 tablespoons heavy cream or
    unsalted butter, optional
Sugar, if needed
Extra-virgin olive oil

1. Preheat the oven to 400°F.

2. Cut the butternut squashes in half lengthwise. Scoop out and discard the seeds. Place the squash halves cut-side up on a rimmed baking sheet. Divide the butter among the hollowed-out seed cavities and generously season the squash with salt and pepper. Lay 1 to 2 strips of bacon lengthwise along the surface of each half. Roast in the oven for 35 to 40 minutes, until a thin-bladed, sharp knife pierces them easily.

3. Remove the baking sheet from the oven. Transfer the bacon to a paper-towel-lined plate to drain. Once cool, mince or crumble into small bits and set aside. Once the squash have cooled slightly, scoop out the flesh with a tablespoon. Reserve the flesh and discard the skins.

4. Heat the olive oil in a large, heavy-bottomed pot over medium-high heat until hot but not smoking. Add the onion, season with salt and pepper, and cook, stirring, until softened but not browned, about 5 minutes. Stir in the thyme sprigs and bay leaf, and then add the squash. Cook, stirring to integrate the flavors and keep the squash from scorching, for 1 to 2 minutes.

5. Add the broth to the pot, stirring to incorporate, and bring to a boil over high heat. Lower the heat and simmer the soup for 15 minutes.

6. Use tongs or a slotted spoon to fish out and discard the thyme sprigs and bay leaf. Transfer the soup to a food processor. (This is one case where I do not recommend an immersion blender because the sheer volume of squash is more easily handled with a processor. If you'd like to use a regular blender, work in batches, and follow the safety tips on page 23.) Add the cream, if using, and process for several minutes until uniformly thick and creamy, but be careful to not turn this voluptuous beauty into a thin soup by overblending! If not serving immediately, let cool, cover, and refrigerate for a few days or freeze for up to 1 month.

7. Return the soup to the pot and gently reheat it. Taste and adjust the seasoning with salt, pepper, and sugar if necessary.

8. To serve, ladle some soup into each of 8 bowls and scatter some of the minced bacon over the surface. Top with thyme leaves and a drizzle of extra-virgin olive oil. Serve at once.

Squash Puree

Squash puree is a colorful, autumn alternative to mashed potatoes and makes a fine companion to Chicken Braised with Mushrooms (page 154) or Duck with Dried Fruits (page 162). For enough puree to serve 8 as a side dish, omit the broth, and add 2 tablespoons cold, unsalted butter to the puree as it's blended in the food processor in Step 6. You can season the puree with a few pinches or dashes of light brown sugar, maple syrup, ground cinnamon, allspice, or nutmeg, according to your own taste.

Tomato, Bread, and Parmesan Soup

◾ Serves 8 ◾

A beguiling and seamless blend of tomatoes, bread, and broth, tomato-and-bread soup is a robust, soulful dish. It's one of those classic Italian preparations that make use of foods that have outlived their usefulness for most people, in this case stale bread and overripe tomatoes.

My tomato-and-bread soup is made deliberately thick with sourdough bread, which is not the conventional choice, but whose distinct flavor goes well with tomatoes and lots of grated Parmigiano-Reggiano cheese. If you've ever read in cookbooks that you should save Parmesan rinds for another use, this is the ultimate one—the rind infuses the entire soup with an authentic Italian flavor.

I make this recipe at the height of tomato season in late summer, when tomatoes are so ripe they crack open. But you can turn to other resources in the winter (see page 245).

4 pounds very ripe beefsteak or Jersey
    tomatoes, peeled (page 245) and
    cut into 1-inch cubes
Coarse salt
Freshly ground black pepper
Sugar
One 8-ounce block Parmigiano-
    Reggiano cheese
¼ cup olive oil, plus more for serving
½ medium Spanish onion, peeled and
    cut into small dice
1 stalk celery, cut into small dice

1 heaping tablespoon tomato paste
2 quarts store-bought, reduced-sodium
    vegetable broth or homemade
    Vegetable Stock (page 244)
1 large loaf or 2 small loaves day-old
    (or two- or three-day-old)
    sourdough or peasant bread, crust
    discarded, cut into 1-inch cubes
    (about 8 cups)
Basil Oil (page 229) or Pesto
    (page 228), optional

1. Thirty minutes before you want to cook, put the tomatoes and their liquid in a bowl and season with salt, pepper, and a pinch of sugar. Grate the cheese and reserve the rind and cheese separately.

2. Heat the olive oil in a large, heavy-bottomed pot over medium-high heat until hot but not yet smoking. Add the onion and celery and cook, stirring frequently, until the vegetables soften, about 5 minutes. Add the tomato paste and a pinch of sugar and cook for 2 minutes, stirring to coat the vegetables.

3. Add the broth and the cheese rind and bring to a boil over high heat. Add the tomatoes with their liquid. Season with salt and pepper and cook, stirring, until the tomatoes begin to liquefy and the soup returns to a boil.

4. Lower the heat and simmer until the tomatoes break down completely and the soup begins to thicken, about 40 minutes. Remove and discard the cheese rind. Add the bread cubes and cook, stirring to break them down, for about 15 minutes. If not serving immediately, let cool, cover, and refrigerate for a few days or freeze for up to 1 month. Reheat before proceeding.

5. Stir in the grated cheese until the soup becomes as thick and flavorful as you like. Personally, I like it as thick as porridge with lots of cheesy flavor; I'd use about a cup of grated cheese. But if you like a lighter touch, feel free to hold back on the cheese.

6. To serve, ladle the soup into individual bowls, hot or at room temperature, garnishing each serving with a few grinds of black pepper, a drizzle of olive oil, and extra grated cheese, if available. You can also top each serving with basil oil or pesto, if desired.

Lemon and Egg Drop Soup

■ Serves 8 ■

Avgolemono is a classic Greek soup, made with chicken broth, lemon, egg, and rice. When made well, you should be able to taste all of the ingredients—the chicken flavor of the broth, the acidity of the lemon, the richness of the egg, and the starch of the rice—in every spoonful. It's another one of those soups that knows countless variations, some using chopped chicken, some using one type of rice, some another, and so on. But in any version, I'm counting on you to do some careful tasting because there's a fine line between bright and lemony and too damn tart. Add the lemon juice in small increments until you achieve the perfect balance. (The strength of flavor will depend on the individual lemons and how fresh they are.)

Since eggs don't react well when reheated, this is a rare exception to the make-ahead convenience of soup—cook this one to order. This is another recipe that would benefit tremendously from the use of homemade stock.

2 quarts homemade Chicken Stock (page 244) or store-bought, reduced-sodium chicken broth	**3 large eggs, at room temperature**
	Juice of 4 large lemons
	Coarse salt
2 cups long-grain rice (page 212)	**Freshly ground black pepper**

1. Bring the stock to a simmer in a large, heavy-bottomed pot over medium heat. Add the rice and bring to a boil over high heat. Lower the heat, cover, and simmer until the rice is just cooked, about 30 minutes.

2. In a large stainless-steel or ceramic bowl, whisk together the eggs and about two thirds of the lemon juice. Season with salt and pepper.

3. Slowly drizzle a cup or 2 of the simmering stock into the bowl with the lemon-egg mixture, whisking to keep the eggs from cooking. Slowly pour this mixture into the pot of simmering stock, whisking until the liquid returns to the simmer. Keep cooking and whisking over medium-low heat until the soup thickens, about 5 minutes. Taste and add more lemon juice as needed.

4. To serve, ladle some soup into each of 8 bowls.

VARIATIONS

Lemon, Egg Drop, and Chicken Soup

If you have some leftover roasted chicken (page 150), shred the meat and add 1 to 2 cups of it to the soup in the final 2 minutes of cooking for a more substantial dish.

Lemon, Egg Drop, and Crabmeat Soup

If you want to make a more elegant dish, purchase some crabmeat, pick through it for shell fragments, place a tablespoon or two in the bottom of each bowl, and ladle the hot soup over it. The crabmeat will be warm by the time the soup is served.

Lemon, Egg Drop, and Spinach Soup

Rinse 1 bunch (about 10 ounces) spinach in several changes of cold water. Cut off and discard the stalks, dry the leaves in a salad spinner or with paper towels, and coarsely chop them. Heat 2 tablespoons olive oil in a sauté pan set over medium-high heat. Add 1 clove minced garlic and cook, stirring, for 30 seconds. Add the spinach, season with salt and pepper, and cook until nicely wilted, about 2 minutes. Stir the spinach into the finished soup just before serving. If preparing the spinach in advance, spread out the cooked spinach on a baking sheet to allow it to cool quickly and prevent it from overcooking and losing its beautiful color.

Potato and Leek Soup

■ Serves 8 ■

It's tough to go wrong with either potatoes or leeks; I love both cooked almost any way. So, as far as I'm concerned, there's much to anticipate when they're combined. This Irish staple (yes, it originated in Ireland, where leeks are about as plentiful as potatoes) proves the point. Seasoning is always important, but you really need to hit it right on the nose here: You should be able to discern both the potatoes and the fresh, light, onion flavor of the leeks.

This soup can be served hot or cold.

3 tablespoons unsalted butter

4 large leeks, white part plus 3 inches of green, split lengthwise, diced, and washed well

2 large Spanish onions, peeled and coarsely chopped

Coarse salt

Freshly ground black pepper

2 cloves garlic, smashed and peeled

3 sprigs thyme

1 bay leaf

2 quarts store-bought, reduced-sodium vegetable or chicken broth, homemade Vegetable or Chicken Stock (page 244), or water

2 pounds baking potatoes (about 3 medium potatoes)

Fried Oysters (page 234), Fried Shallots (page 235), or Frizzled Leeks (page 236), optional

1. Melt the butter in a large, heavy-bottomed pot with at least a 4-quart capacity (the leeks take up a lot of space until they cook down) over medium heat. Add the leeks and onions, season with salt and pepper, and cook, stirring often, until the vegetables are softened, 10 to 12 minutes.

2. Add the garlic, thyme, and bay leaf. Stir well to integrate the flavors. Pour in the broth and bring to a boil over high heat. Reduce the heat and simmer for about 30 minutes.

3. While the broth is simmering, peel the potatoes and cut them into 1-inch dice. Put them in a bowl and cover with cold water. Set aside.

4. Drain the potatoes, add to the pot, and return the liquid to a boil over high heat. Reduce the heat and simmer until the potatoes are tender when pierced with a thin-bladed, sharp knife, about 20 minutes.

5. Use tongs or a slotted spoon to fish out and discard the thyme sprigs and bay leaf. Working in batches, puree the soup in a blender until thick and creamy (see safety tips, page 23). Season with salt and pepper. If not serving immediately, or if you want to serve cold, let cool, cover, and refrigerate for a few days or freeze for up to 1 month. If serving hot, reheat before proceeding.

6. To serve, ladle some soup into each of 8 bowls and top with fried oysters, fried shallots, or frizzled leeks, if desired.

VARIATIONS

Sweet, Spring Onion Soup

For an irresistibly sweet and decidedly light soup, replace the leeks with 3 pounds of beautiful, bulbing spring onions.

(Mashed) Potato and Leek Soup

At Ouest, we take this recipe to new levels of spud-dom by mounding some mashed potatoes in the center of shallow soup bowls and ladling the soup around it. If you have, or feel like making, Mashed Potatoes (page 221), you should do the same, and top the dish with Fried Oysters (page 234) as embellishment. Only do this if serving the soup hot.

Twice-Cooked Vegetable Soup

■ *Serves 8* ■

The Italian *ribollita* (the name means "twice-boiled") is one of a diverse family of Italian soups known as *zuppe di pane,* or bread soups, because they are spooned over a fried crouton in the bottom of the bowl. I love the way these disparate ingredients break down during the long, slow cooking process and create a compelling, composite vegetable flavor; just try to tell where one flavor ends and another begins—it's practically impossible. This effect is reinforced so much by time that letting it sit overnight is part of the original recipe.

I like to add extra flavor by melting some grated Parmesan on the crouton and finishing the soup with a generous amount of chopped, fresh basil or parsley. You can also add extra flavor by drizzling some Basil Oil (page 229) or Pesto (page 228) over each serving.

If you don't want to go to the trouble of peeling tomatoes, use canned tomatoes instead of fresh.

¾ cup olive oil

2 large carrots, peeled and cut into ¼-inch rounds

1 large Spanish onion, peeled and cut into small dice

1 large leek, white part plus 1 inch of green, thinly sliced and washed well

2 stalks celery, cut crosswise into ¼-inch pieces

2 cloves garlic, smashed and peeled

Coarse salt

Freshly ground black pepper

2 medium Yukon Gold potatoes, peeled and cut into ¼-inch dice

4 plum tomatoes, peeled (page 245), or 4 whole, canned tomatoes, drained

½ head Savoy cabbage, core removed, coarsely chopped

1 bunch kale, stems and tough center stalks removed, coarsely chopped

One 15-ounce can cannellini beans, rinsed and drained

2 quarts store-bought, reduced-sodium vegetable or chicken broth or homemade Vegetable or Chicken Stock (page 244)

Eight 1-inch-thick slices white peasant
   or country bread
1 to 1½ cups freshly grated Parmesan
   cheese

1 cup loosely packed, chopped fresh
   basil or parsley leaves or Pesto
   (page 228), optional

1. Heat 2 tablespoons of the olive oil in a large, heavy-bottomed pot over medium-high heat until hot but not smoking. Add the carrots, onion, leek, celery, and garlic, season with salt and pepper, and cook, stirring, until the vegetables are softened but not brown, about 5 minutes.

2. Add the potatoes, stir to let them soak up the flavor of the other vegetables, and cook for 2 to 3 minutes. Add the tomatoes, cabbage, kale, and beans. Season with salt and pepper and cook, stirring, for 2 to 3 minutes. Pour the broth into the pot, stir gently, and bring to a boil over high heat. Lower the heat, cover, and simmer for 2 hours.

3. Remove the pot from the heat and let the soup cool. Cover and refrigerate for at least overnight or for up to a few days, or freeze for up to 1 month.

4. When ready to proceed, preheat the oven to 400°F. Return the soup to the pot and gently reheat it.

5. While the soup is warming, lay the slices of bread on a baking sheet and brush both sides with the remaining olive oil. Toast in the oven until browned, about 5 minutes, then turn and brown on the other side. Remove the baking sheet from the oven and preheat the broiler. Top each bread slice with some grated Parmesan. Place under the broiler until the cheese melts and is bubbly, about 2 minutes.

6. To serve, place one cheese crouton in the center of each of 6 bowls. Stir the basil, parsley, or pesto, if using, into the soup. Ladle some soup over the crouton in each bowl. Serve at once, passing any remaining grated cheese on the side.

CAVOLO NERO

Most Tuscans will tell you to make this recipe with *cavolo nero* or black cabbage, a vegetable that is all but impossible to find in the United States. If you can get it from a gourmet grocer or farmers' market, or grow it yourself, by all means use it to replace the kale.

Extra-Smoky New England Clam Chowder

■ *Serves 6* ■

Without a doubt, my favorite thing about New England clam chowder is the salt pork that flavors the entire soup. In this recipe, I turn to my preferred version of this ingredient, double-smoked bacon, which permeates the rich cream. Unlike many chowders, this one encourages you to leave the bacon in when you serve the soup. It can also be made ahead, provided you don't add the cream until reheating. To really push this soup over the top, float a few Fried Oysters (page 234) on the surface of each serving.

2 cups dry white wine
Coarse salt
Freshly ground black pepper
4 pounds small clams (page 49)
½ pound double-smoked bacon
    (page 241), cut into ¼-inch dice
2 large leeks, white part only,
    quartered lengthwise, thinly sliced,
    and washed well

1 large Spanish onion, peeled and cut
    into small dice
2 tablespoons all-purpose flour
1½ pounds Yukon Gold Potatoes,
    peeled and cut into ¼-inch dice
1 quart heavy cream, or 2 cups cream
    and 2 cups whole milk

1. Pour the wine into a large pot and season it with salt and pepper. Place the pot over high heat and warm the wine for 1 to 2 minutes.

2. Add the clams to the pot, cover, and cook until they open, about 5 minutes. Remove the pot from the heat and use tongs or a slotted spoon to transfer the clams to a large bowl. Set aside to cool. Discard any clams that have not opened. Strain and reserve the cooking liquid in a bowl.

3. When the clams are cool enough to handle, remove them from their shells, if desired. Discard the shells and set the clams aside.

4. Wipe out the pot. Add the bacon and cook over low heat until it renders enough fat to coat the bottom of the pot generously, about 5 minutes. Add the leeks and onion, season with salt and pepper, and cook until softened but not browned, about 5 minutes. Add the flour and stir until the leeks and onion are well coated.

5. Pour in the reserved clam cooking liquid and add the potatoes. If the liquid does not cover the potatoes, add enough water just to cover them. Give a good but gentle stir, raise the heat, and bring to a boil. Lower the heat, cover, and simmer until the potatoes are just tender but still a bit al dente, about 15 minutes. If not serving immediately, let cool, cover, and refrigerate for a few days or freeze for up to 1 month. Reheat before proceeding.

6. Stir in the cream and cook until warmed through; do not boil. Taste and adjust the seasoning if necessary.

7. To serve, ladle some soup into each of 6 bowls.

VARIATION

Smoked Cod Chowder

For a sensational variation to this recipe, omit the clams and wine and start with Step 4. Add 1½ cups bottled clam juice in Step 5. Flake ½ pound smoked cod (see Mail-Order Sources, page 247) at room temperature, into the soup 1 minute before serving.

CLAMS

As a general rule, if I'm making a dish in which clams are eaten whole, I use those that aren't much bigger in diameter than a ping-pong ball, such as Manila clams, mahogany clams, and a close relative, New Zealand cockles. If, on the other hand, the clams are going to be chopped, I use cherrystone or littleneck clams.

To clean clams, fill a large bowl halfway with cold water and salt it well. Add the clams, agitate them gently, and let soak in the refrigerator for 2 hours. This will draw out the grit. To remove any dirt stuck to the shell, scrub them under cold running water with a towel or a brush reserved for this and other foods (in other words, don't use the same brush you use to clean your sink).

Ironically, I don't include chowder clams in any dishes, not even chowder, because I find them too tough regardless of how much you cook or chop them. But their flavor is exceptional and makes a potent clam broth. For each pound of chowder clams, heat ½ cup dry white wine (or water) in a stockpot with 1 clove smashed and peeled garlic. Add the clams, cover, and cook until they pop open, about 5 minutes. Then, discard the clams and strain the broth. Use it to add flavor to fish stew, soups, and pasta sauces by replacing some of the liquid in a recipe with the clam broth. (I freeze clam broth in ice-cube trays then transfer the cubes to an airtight bag so I can defrost only as much as I need at any given time.)

Mussel Chowder

■ Serves 8 ■

When most people hear the word *chowder*, they immediately think of clams. But I'm hard-pressed to choose between the briny flavor of clams and the relatively sweet quality of mussels, which I like in a brothy Manhattan-style chowder with tomatoes, diced potato, and herbs. (This recipe also makes a great clam chowder by simply substituting clams for mussels.) You can leave the mussels in their shells for a dramatic presentation, or remove the shells from all or half of them.

Serve this with croutons spread with Saffron Aïoli (page 231) or Red Pepper Aïoli (page 230).

6 plum tomatoes, cut into 1-inch cubes
Coarse salt
Freshly ground black pepper
Sugar
1 cup dry white wine
8 cloves garlic, 2 smashed and peeled and 6 peeled and thinly sliced
3 pounds mussels, scrubbed and debearded (page 53)
1 teaspoon olive oil
6 ounces double-smoked bacon (page 241), cut into small dice (about 1½ cups)
1 large carrot, peeled and cut into small dice

1 large Spanish onion, peeled and cut into small dice
2 celery stalks, cut into small dice
3 tablespoons tomato paste
1 medium, or 2 small, Yukon Gold potatoes, peeled and cut into ½-inch cubes
1 teaspoon chopped fresh thyme leaves
1 bay leaf
3 cups store-bought, reduced-sodium chicken broth or homemade Chicken Stock (page 244)

1. About 30 minutes before you want to cook, put the tomatoes in a bowl and season with salt, pepper, and a pinch of sugar. Set aside.

2. Pour the wine into a large pot, add the smashed garlic, and season with salt and pepper. Bring the wine to a boil over high heat. Add the mussels to the pot, cover, and

cook until they open, about 5 minutes. Remove the pot from the heat and use tongs or a slotted spoon to transfer the mussels to a large bowl. Discard any mussels that do not open. Set aside to cool. Strain and reserve the cooking liquid in a bowl. (You should have about 1 cup of liquid.)

3. When the mussels are cool enough to handle, remove them from their shells, if desired. Discard the shells and set the mussels aside.

4. Wipe out the pot. Add the olive oil and bacon and cook over medium-high heat until the bacon begins to render its fat, about 5 minutes. Add the carrot, onion, celery, and sliced garlic to the pot. Cook, stirring occasionally, until the vegetables start to soften, 2 to 3 minutes.

5. Add the tomato paste to the pot and stir to coat the vegetables with the paste. Cook, stirring, for another 3 to 4 minutes. Add the potatoes, thyme, bay leaf, and tomatoes and their juice to the pot and cook for 3 minutes.

6. Pour the broth and reserved mussel cooking liquid into the pot. Bring to a boil over high heat. Lower the heat, taste, and season with salt and pepper if necessary. Simmer until the potatoes are nearly tender, about 15 minutes. If not serving immediately, let cool, cover, and refrigerate the mussels and soup separately for 1 or 2 days. Reheat the soup before proceeding.

7. Add the mussels and heat gently for 5 minutes. To serve, ladle some of the soup into each of 6 bowls.

VARIATIONS

Clam Chowder

If you don't love mussels, substitute clams (page 49).

Oyster Chowder

For oyster chowder, omit the clams and wine and add ½ cup bottled clam juice in Step 6 to make up for the missing cooking liquid. Poach 24 shucked oysters in the simmering soup for 1 to 2 minutes before serving.

MUSSELS

Most mussels available in markets today are cultivated, which consequently means they don't have as much flavor as wild ones but are nonetheless sweet and delicious and offer consistent quality. They should be scrubbed under cold running water and their beards (the hairy thread by which they attach themselves to rocks or other hosts) should be removed before they are cooked. If you're cooking with very fresh mussels, the beard may be hard to remove prior to cooking; if so, remove it afterwards.

Most markets in the United States sell cultivated blue mussels. If you can find them, I prefer Prince Edward Island mussels which are uniformly small with tightly closed black shells. Less commonly available but worth seeking out are the stupendous New Zealand green (or green-lipped) mussel. These are about twice the size of other mussels and have a beautiful green tint to the shell. They're delicate and superior in flavor.

Mussels with Tomato and Saffron

Serves 6

When you steam mussels, so much broth is produced that I think of what's in the pot as a sort of soup. That observation led to this recipe, in which the steaming liquid is a more complex soup base featuring sautéed garlic, tomatoes, clam juice, and wine. The mussels provide the final ingredient—that sweet, briny juice given off when they steam open completes the soup.

Serve this with croutons spread with Saffron Aïoli (page 231).

¼ cup olive oil
4 garlic cloves, smashed and peeled
2 bay leaves
Pinch of saffron threads (page 55)
2 plum tomatoes, seeded (page 245)
   and diced
1 cup bottled clam juice

½ cup dry white wine
6 pounds mussels, scrubbed and
   debearded (page 53)
¼ teaspoon crushed red pepper
3 tablespoons minced fresh flat-leaf
   parsley leaves

1. Divide the olive oil between 2 large pots and warm over medium-high heat. Add 1 garlic clove to each pot and sauté for 2 to 3 minutes. Add a bay leaf and half of the saffron to each pot, stir to coat with oil, and cook for 1 minute.

2. Add half the tomatoes, clam juice, and wine to each pot. Raise the heat and bring to a boil. Lower the heat, cover, and simmer for 20 minutes.

3. Remove the covers, add half the mussels to each pot, raise the heat, and cook, covered, until the mussels open, about 5 minutes. Use tongs or a slotted spoon to transfer the mussels to a large bowl. Fish out and discard the bay leaves and any mussels that have not opened. Combine the liquids in one of the pots, add the crushed red pepper and parsley, and stir to incorporate.

4. Divide the mussels among 6 soup bowls and ladle some soup over them. Serve at once.

Mussels with White Wine and Scallion

For a broth with more bite, omit the saffron and add 2 thinly sliced scallions along with the garlic in Step 1.

Mussels with Ginger, Scallion, and Cilantro

Add 2 thinly sliced scallions and 1 tablespoon grated fresh ginger along with the garlic in Step 1. For an extra, Asian tang, add a splash of rice vinegar with the wine in Step 2. Add ½ cup coarsely chopped cilantro leaves after removing the mussels from the pot in Step 4. This version can be made even more substantial with the addition of precooked rice noodles just before serving.

TOMORROW'S TABLE

Mussel Salad

If you have leftover mussels, refrigerate them and their cooking liquid separately in airtight containers. Whisk 4½ teaspoons freshly squeezed lemon juice and 1½ teaspoons Dijon mustard into ½ cup mayonnaise (page 230). Put the mussels in a bowl with a few tablespoons of reserved cooking liquid. Add the mayonnaise and toss gently. Serve on a bed of Bibb lettuce or in pitted avocado halves, dressed with a squeeze of lemon juice, a drizzle of olive oil, and a sprinkling of salt and pepper.

SAFFRON

Saffron is widely known as the most expensive spice in the world, and there's good reason for this: Tens of thousands of flowers have to be hand-picked to gather just one pound of the stuff. (The spice is made from the dried stigmas of the purple saffron crocus.) Look for the wonderfully useful, small packages of saffron available in many markets today. You can buy just as much as you need, which in this case is only a pinch. I've always found that saffron makes a great gift for home cooks: A lot of people don't keep it on hand, a little goes a long way, and every time they reach for it, they'll think of you.

Lobster Bisque

■ Serves 6 ■

Lobster bisque sounds old-fashioned, and it is. The recipe predates me and everyone reading this. But it's one of those classics that will probably never fade away because it's got so much going for it. Few foods are as special as lobster, and the idea of digging into a cream-based soup built around the flavor of this crustacean is irresistible. My recipe for lobster bisque essentially expands the recipe I use at Ouest to make lobster stock with the addition of cream, herbs, and rice. Classic bisque recipes also feature Cognac, but I prefer to keep the focus on the lobster.

4 live lobsters, (about 1 pound each)
3 tablespoons olive oil
¼ cup tomato paste
2 plum tomatoes, coarsely chopped
2 sprigs tarragon plus 2 tablespoons
   tarragon leaves
2 sprigs flat-leaf parsley
2 sprigs thyme
2 cloves garlic, peeled and thinly sliced

⅓ cup dry white wine
2 teaspoons distilled white vinegar
   (page 246)
3 cups heavy cream
Pinch of sugar
1 tablespoon black peppercorns
1½ cups cooked, long-grain rice (from
   ¾ cup uncooked rice, page 212)

1. Bring a stockpot of salted water to a boil over high heat. Fill a large bowl halfway with ice water and set aside.

2. Carefully lower the lobsters into the pot, cover, and cook for 5 minutes. Turn off the heat and let the lobsters sit in the covered pot for another minute. Use tongs to remove the lobsters from the pot and submerge them in the ice water until well chilled. Take the head in one hand and the tail in the other and twist them in opposite directions until the upper and lower halves come apart. Split the lobster tail in half lengthwise with a large knife. Remove the lobster meat from the tail and body. Crack the claws and remove the meat from within. Cut the meat into small dice and set it aside. Remove the gray-green tomalley (liver) and red roe (if there is any) from the lobster. Reserve the meat, shells, and tomalley with the roe in separate airtight containers in the refrigerator. This step can be performed up to 24 hours ahead of time. Let come to room temperature before proceeding.

3. Heat the oil in a heavy-bottomed pot over high heat until hot but not yet smoking. Add the lobster shells (be careful, they will spit) and cook for 2 to 3 minutes. Reduce the heat to low, add the tomato paste and stir to coat the lobster. Cook for 2 to 3 minutes longer.

4. In a small bowl, combine the reserved roe (if any) and tomalley with the tomatoes, tarragon sprigs, parsley, thyme, and garlic.

5. Pour the white wine and vinegar into the pot. Add the tomato mixture, the cream to cover the shells, the peppercorns, 1 teaspoon of salt, and a pinch of sugar.

6. Simmer gently over medium heat for 15 minutes. (Do not let the cream boil.) Taste the broth. If the lobster flavor has not yet infused the broth, cook for another 5 minutes. (Pay special attention here. If overcooked, this can take on an unpleasant, murky flavor. As soon as you taste the lobster cleanly and deliciously, stop cooking.)

7. Strain the broth into a bowl and discard the solids. You should have 2½ to 3 cups of liquid. If not serving immediately, let cool, cover, and refrigerate for a few days or freeze for up to 1 month. Reheat gently before proceeding.

8. Return the bisque to the pot. Stir in the rice and tarragon leaves. Warm over low heat.

9. To serve, ladle some soup into each of 6 shallow bowls and garnish with the lobster meat.

VARIATIONS

Shrimp Bisque

Make a shrimp bisque by replacing the lobster with 3 pounds of large shrimp. Be sure to purchase the shrimp with the shells intact. Remove the shells and set aside. Clean and butterfly the shrimp (see page 87) and set aside. Make the bisque using the shrimp shells in place of the lobster shells, but only cook them for 30 to 40 seconds in Step 3. Gently poach the shrimp in the simmering soup in Step 6 for a few minutes, until firm and pink, just before serving.

Linguine with Lobster or Shrimp

Make this recipe (or the Shrimp Bisque variation) using only ½ cup of cream for a powerfully flavored pasta sauce. Cook 1 pound fresh linguine in salted boiling water until al dente, 2 to 3 minutes. Drain the pasta and toss it with the sauce. Top with lots of freshly chopped tomato and basil.

Tuscan-Style Seafood Stew

▓ Serves 4 ▓

Have you ever eaten food in Europe and then tried to enjoy the same dish in the United States, only to be disappointed? Well, *cacciucco,* the Tuscan fish stew, and *bouillabaisse,* its French cousin, are two dishes that often elicit this reaction. The primary reason is that an ingredient crucial to both soups—scorpionfish or *racasse rouge*—is difficult to find on this side of the Atlantic. But this recipe, by using two relatively oily fish (bluefish and mackerel), creates a flavor that comes pretty close.

1¼ cups olive oil

8 cloves garlic, peeled and coarsely chopped

1 large carrot, peeled and coarsely chopped

1 small red onion, peeled and minced

½ teaspoon crushed red pepper

Coarse salt

Freshly ground black pepper

¾ cup minced flat-leaf parsley leaves

1 pound skinless cod fillet, cut into 1-inch cubes

1 cup dry white wine

½ cup distilled white vinegar (page 246)

4 cups coarsely chopped canned plum tomatoes (about 8 tomatoes)

8 ounces skinless bluefish, cut into 1-inch cubes

8 ounces skinless mackerel, cut into 1-inch cubes

8 ounces skinless swordfish, cut into 1-inch cubes

8 ounces sea scallops

8 ounces mussels, scrubbed and debearded (page 53)

8 ounces small clams, cleaned and scrubbed (page 49)

12 slices 1-inch-thick country or peasant bread

1. Preheat the oven to 400°F.

2. Heat ½ cup of the olive oil in a heavy-bottomed pot large enough to hold all the ingredients over medium heat until hot but not smoking. Add the garlic, carrot, onion, and crushed red pepper, season with salt and pepper, and cook, stirring occasionally, until the onion is lightly browned, about 7 minutes. Add ½ cup of the parsley and stir to combine.

3. Add half the cod (which will break down and help thicken the broth), along with the wine, and simmer until the wine reduces by two-thirds, about 5 minutes. Stir in the vinegar and tomatoes and simmer for 10 minutes.

4. Add the remaining cod, the bluefish, mackerel, swordfish, and scallops. Season with salt and pepper and give a gentle stir. Then add the mussels and clams, letting them rest on top of the stew. Cover the pot and simmer gently until the mussels and clams have opened, 5 to 10 minutes.

5. While the mussels are steaming, lay the slices of bread on a baking sheet and brush both sides with the remaining olive oil. Toast in the oven until browned, about 5 minutes, then turn and brown on the other side. Remove the baking sheet from the oven.

6. Ladle some soup into each of 4 bowls and place a few clams and mussels on top of each serving. Sprinkle some of the remaining ¼ cup parsley over each bowl. Serve each portion with 3 slices of fried bread.

VARIATIONS

Seafood Pasta

For an unusual seafood pasta, toss the stew with cooked angel hair pasta. A 1-pound box will stretch this to serve up to 8 people.

TOMORROW'S TABLE

Bouillabaisse Soup

Take any leftover soup from Tuscany to the West Coast of France: Remove any remaining clams and puree the soup in a food processor. When you reheat the soup over low heat, add a pinch of saffron threads (see note, page 55) or a splash of Pernod—or both—and stir in 2 tablespoons of extra-virgin olive oil. Serve with ½-inch rounds cut from a baguette, toasted, and spread with Aïoli (page 230).

Spicy Shellfish Soup

Serves 6

I simply adore soups and stews that feature the trio of shellfish, tomatoes, and spicy crushed red pepper flakes. You can vary the selection of shellfish in this recipe, but be sure to use a good mix of types and sizes; the variation makes for a more complex flavor and the different shells offer a dramatic presentation. As with all shellfish soups, do not to let the liquid boil when the fish is in the pot; a gentle simmer is essential to prevent the meat from overcooking and becoming rubbery.

Serve this with croutons spread with Red Pepper Aïoli (page 230) or drizzle some Basil Oil (page 229) over each serving.

2 tablespoons olive oil

1 large carrot, peeled and cut into small dice

1 large Spanish onion, peeled and cut into small dice

3 cloves garlic, peeled and thinly sliced

Coarse salt

Freshly ground black pepper

2 tablespoons tomato paste

1 large, ripe beefsteak tomato, seeded (page 245) and cut into 1-inch cubes

1 cup dry white wine

2 teaspoons distilled white vinegar (page 246)

Pinch of saffron threads (page 55)

Pinch of crushed red pepper, or more to taste

1 bay leaf

2 tablespoons chopped fresh marjoram or oregano leaves

1 quart store-bought, reduced-sodium vegetable broth or homemade Vegetable Stock (page 244)

1 to 1½ pounds mixed shellfish: mussels (page 53), small clams (page 49), or cockles in their shells; bay scallops; or medium or large shrimp, preferably fresh, head on, and in their shells

1. Heat the olive oil in a large, heavy-bottomed pot over medium-high heat until hot but not smoking. Add the carrot, onion, and garlic, season with salt and black pepper, and cook, stirring, until the vegetables soften, about 5 minutes. Add the tomato paste and stir well to coat the vegetables. Continue to cook for 2 minutes. Add the tomato to the pot, season with salt and pepper, and cook, stirring, for 3 minutes.

2. Turn the heat up to high. Add the white wine and vinegar to the pot and cook for 3 to 4 minutes, stirring with a wooden spoon to loosen any bits of tomato and vegetable that might be stuck to the bottom of the pot. Add the saffron, crushed red pepper, bay leaf, and marjoram to the pot and give a good stir to integrate the flavors. Pour in the broth, season with salt and pepper, and bring to a boil. Lower the heat and simmer for 10 to 15 minutes.

3. Add the shellfish in the following order: First add the mussels and clams, making sure to immerse them in the liquid. Cover the pot and simmer until they pop open, about 5 minutes. Immediately add the other shellfish, also immersing them in the liquid, and simmer, uncovered, for 6 to 7 minutes. Taste the soup and adjust the seasoning with salt, pepper, and crushed red pepper if necessary. Use tongs or a slotted spoon to fish out and discard the bay leaf as well as any mussels or clams that have not opened.

4. Transfer a good variety of shellfish to each of 6 bowls and ladle soup over the top.

Turkey Soup with Stuffing Dumplings

Creatively using leftovers is one of the highlights of every Thanksgiving weekend and this soup is one of my favorite ways to use everything, from the turkey bones to a surplus of vegetables, herbs, and meat. But the most unusual touch here is making dumplings out of leftover stuffing. Not to pat myself on the back, but I've never seen anyone else do this, and I think it's delicious. This recipe can be adapted for as many leftovers (and family members) as you have on hand after the Thanksgiving meal is done (see the note at the end of the recipe). You can also add barley (page 207) or wild rice (page 213) in addition to, or in place of, the dumplings. Because these take much longer to cook, precook them following the instructions on pages 207 and 213.

Carcass from a roasted turkey, hacked into large pieces with a meat cleaver or large, heavy knife

1 large carrot, peeled and coarsely chopped

1 large Spanish onion, peeled and coarsely chopped

1 stalk celery, peeled and coarsely chopped

1 large leek, white part plus 1 inch of green, coarsely chopped, and washed well

1 tablespoon black peppercorns

Coarse salt

1 large egg yolk, beaten

Freshly ground black pepper

1 tablespoon chopped fresh herbs, such as thyme, parsley, or sage, or a combination, plus more for serving, optional

1 cup leftover stuffing

1 cup chopped, leftover turkey

1 cup chopped leftover cooked vegetables such as onion, carrot, or celery, or a combination, optional

1. Put the turkey carcass pieces, raw carrot, onion, celery, leek, peppercorns, and 1 tablespoon of salt in a stockpot and add enough water to cover by 2 inches. Bring to a boil over medium-high heat, then lower the heat and simmer for 2 to 4 hours, skimming off any foam that rises to the surface during this time. The soup will be ready after 2 hours, but will intensify in turkey flavor as it continues to simmer. Taste frequently and remove from the heat when you are satisfied.

2. While the soup is simmering, prepare the dumplings. Put the egg yolk in a large bowl and season lightly with salt and pepper. Add the herbs and beat well. Add the stuffing and stir gently but thoroughly to combine. Remove a tablespoon of batter at a time and form it into a ball-shaped dumpling between the palms of your hands. Set on a large plate. Repeat until all the batter has been used. Cover the plate loosely with plastic wrap and refrigerate for up to 24 hours.

3. Strain the soup through a fine-mesh strainer set over a large bowl. Discard the solids. If not serving immediately, let cool, cover, and refrigerate overnight.

4. Wipe out the pot and pour the soup into it. Bring to a gentle boil over medium-high heat. Carefully lower the dumplings into the soup and heat through, about 7 minutes. If desired, add chopped leftover turkey, diced vegetables, or additional chopped herbs during the last 2 minutes of cooking time. Taste and season with salt and pepper.

5. To serve, ladle some soup into each of 6 bowls, making sure to include a few dumplings in each serving.

TO MAKE MORE SOUP

For more soup, add more water before simmering, or add chicken broth to the strained stock in Step 3. For each additional cup of stuffing, add 1 more egg to make the dumplings, and increase the chopped herbs by 1 tablespoon. Add more diced turkey and vegetables as desired.

Ham Hock and Split Pea Soup

■ *Serves 6* ■

Split peas are halved peas, which is obvious. They are also dried peas, which is probably—when you think about it—just as obvious. I mean, have you ever tried to cut a fresh pea in half?

Split peas and ham are meant to go together, so much so that a minimum of supporting ingredients are called for to flesh them out into a satisfying soup.

Most people think of split pea soup as a thick-as-can-be affair, and this is how I like it, but it doesn't need to be. In fact, a thinner version is delicious and more surprising. If you like, add a bit more liquid to thin the soup, and see what you think. (If unsure, you can add some to a cupful of soup at the end and, if you approve, stir more into the pot.)

2 cups green split peas, picked
    through, small stones discarded
2 tablespoons olive oil
1 large carrot, peeled and cut into
    small dice
1 medium Spanish onion, peeled and
    cut into small dice
1 stalk celery, cut into small dice
Coarse salt
Freshly ground black pepper
Sugar
1 large clove garlic, smashed and peeled

1 bay leaf
3 sprigs marjoram or thyme
2 quarts store-bought, reduced-
    sodium vegetable or chicken broth,
    homemade Vegetable or Chicken
    Stock (page 244), water, or a
    combination
2 pounds smoked ham hocks
    (see note, page 67)
Extra-virgin olive oil
2 tablespoons fresh thyme leaves or
    Garlic Croutons (page 233), optional

1. Put the split peas in a bowl and cover with cold water. Set aside.

2. Heat the oil in a large, heavy-bottomed pot over medium heat until hot but not smoking. Add the carrot, onion, and celery; season with salt, pepper, and a pinch of sugar; and cook, stirring, until the vegetables soften, 5 to 7 minutes. Add the garlic and cook for another 2 minutes.

3. Drain the split peas and add them to the pot. Add the bay leaf, marjoram, broth, and ham hocks. Give a good stir and bring the liquid to a boil over high heat, continuing to stir to keep the peas from scorching. Lower the heat, cover, and simmer for 1 hour.

4. Use tongs or a slotted spoon to remove the ham hocks from the pot. Set them aside on a plate. Cook the soup for 30 minutes longer, or until the peas and other vegetables have completely broken down and the soup has thickened considerably. If it becomes *too* thick, add more stock or water (see note).

5. While the soup is simmering, and as soon as the ham hock have cooled enough to work with, use your hands to remove the meat from the bones, shredding it as you work. There won't be a lot of it, but what is there is very flavorful. Set the meat aside.

6. When the soup is done, use tongs or a spoon to remove and discard the bay leaf and marjoram sprigs. Taste and correct seasoning, bearing in mind that the bits of ham are salty. Add the reserved ham to the pot. If not serving immediately, let cool, cover, and refrigerate for a few days or freeze for up to 1 month. Reheat before proceeding.

7. To serve, ladle the soup into individual bowls and drizzle with extra-virgin olive oil. Scatter some thyme leaves over each serving, if desired, or float a garlic crouton on top of each bowl.

HAM HOCKS

A lot of American cooks are unfamiliar with ham hocks, even though they're a staple in the South. I first discovered them as a child when my grandmother took me along on her excursions to the supermarket. While she stood talking to the butcher, my eye would wander over to the refrigerated meats section. For the longest time, I didn't even ask what these funny-looking, prewrapped, precooked, brown things were, but in time I learned that they were smoked ham hocks. They've become one of my favorite incarnations of pork. They're user-friendly and have great utility. They also give off a lot of natural gelatin, which acts as a subtle thickening agent, adding body to soups and sauces.

Casseroles, Stews, and Chili

To some extent, all good food conjures images of friends and loved ones gathered around a table to eat. But when I think about casseroles, stews, and chili, I don't just picture people eating; I envision *big* groups of people engaged in raucous times that last for hours and hours.

To me, dishes like Texas-Style Chili (page 114), Beer and Beef Stew (page 116), and Macaroni and Goat Cheese (page 90) bring to mind fall and winter football parties, with guests moving to and from a buffet table, replenishing their bowls from a seemingly bottomless pot, and returning to the living room to watch the Sunday game. Similarly, Tuna Noodle Casserole (page 94), Spaghetti with Tuna and Tomato (page 93), and Lamb Pasticcio (page 124) make me think of an extended family (Italian-American in my mind's eye) laughing and lingering for hours over a table, drawn there as much by the food as by each other's company.

These are just a few of the reasons the foods in this chapter are universally beloved. Another explanation for their wide appeal is that all are fun-to-eat hodgepodges of textures and flavors—from the meat, beans, and spices in a chili to the tomato, garlic, and seafood in a pasta sauce to the beef, vegetables, and grain in a stew.

What's more, because they feature so many ingredients, these foods offer almost endless opportunity for personalization that can instantly redefine them—as when you adjust the amount of pepper in a chili or alter the selection of vegetables in a stew. Even after they're delivered to the table, these dishes can be adapted to each diner's personal taste, whether by livening up a pasta sauce with crushed red pepper and enriching it with extra-virgin olive oil; topping a risotto with lots of grated Parmesan cheese; or dressing a chili with Tabasco sauce, crushed saltines, sour cream, and cheddar cheese. These are dishes you can practically recreate at the table and not offend the cook.

Here are a few thoughts on the recipes that follow:

Chili

When I think of the best chilis I've had over the years, I have to say that my personal prerequisite for chili is not beef or beans or tomatoes. To me, what's truly essential is that chili is spicy and the heat is interesting. What I mean is that anyone armed with a jar of cayenne pepper or a bottle of Tabasco sauce can make something spicy. The challenge is to make the heat taste *good,* to compose a little three-alarm aria that's compelling from one bite to the next by including ingredients of varying heat levels that deliver wave upon wave of pleasurable punishment to your taste buds. As far as I'm concerned, great chili doesn't truly fade from the palate until about 30 minutes after you're done eating it, like the triumphant, gradual fade-to-black at the end of a great movie.

This means different things to different diners. Like fingerprints, no two people have the same tolerance for heat. When making chili, we have to factor in our audience, especially if it contains that culinary wimp in our lives who can't stand heat at all. You know who I'm talking about; the one who chokes on a generous amount of black pepper in a nonspicy dish.

The best way to accomplish this is to know your peppers and spices, so here are a few notes on those used in the chili recipes that follow. To state the obvious, there are countless peppers out there—many more than I could justify detailing here. I encourage you to explore the wide world of fresh and dried peppers and get to know as many as you can. They will all expand your options—not just when making chili, but whenever you need a little something extra to perk up a sauce or a soup.

Of the peppers I use in this chapter, bell peppers are by far the most commonly available and widely known. They are the peppers you no doubt picture when you hear the word *pepper:* sweet and crunchy, available in colors from green to red to orange to yellow, and mild and flavorful, if not particularly hot.

For a more complex flavor, I turn to one of the most popular items in the Mexican cupboard, dried ancho chile powder, which brings an alluring combination of heat and fruitiness to its surroundings. In contrast, when pure heat is what I'm after, there's no quicker way to get there than cayenne, which is the pepper that fuels red Tabasco sauce and other hot sauces. If you only want to have a few peppers in your pantry, think about creating the overall flavor of a chili with ancho chile powder, then upping the heat level with careful additions of cayenne.

For smoky heat, I turn to chipotle peppers, which are smoked jalapeños. They are sold dried or reconstituted and stored in adobo, a tangy tomato sauce that can be used in chili, soups, and stews as well. One of the things I appreciate most about chipotle peppers in adobo is that they don't need to be reconstituted in the dish, so they taste the same when they go into the pot as they do when they finish cooking. In contrast, most dried peppers reconstitute when cooked, so it's difficult to control their heat.

As for hot sauces, Tabasco is just the beginning. There are innumerable sauces out there and, as with peppers themselves, they reward experimentation. The Tabasco folks have even upped the ante with versions featuring chipotle and hotter 'n hell habanero—the spiciest of all peppers.

Finally, I would be remiss if I didn't mention chili powder, which turns up in most chili recipes, including mine. Chili powder is actually a blend of dried peppers meant for chili-making. Every brand is made according to a different formula, so chili powders lack the consistency of specific dried peppers. When using one, you must taste the chili frequently and adjust the flavor as necessary.

Pasta

All of the pasta recipes in this chapter use dried pasta. There are additional notes on individual pasta shapes on pages 216 to 220, but keep the following general advice in mind when cooking out of this chapter:

Not all pastas are created equal, so find a brand you like. (Let me save you some time: My favorite, and the favorite of just about every chef I know, is De Cecco for its great semolina flavor and perfect thickness in all of the many shapes it sells.) Cook the pasta itself in plenty of boiling, salted water. (The generally accepted formula is six quarts of water and two tablespoons of salt per pound of pasta.) And cook your pasta *al dente* ("to the tooth"), meaning that it still has a bit of a bite to it. I find that if you cut one minute off the recommended cooking time on the box or bag, you'll get pretty close to the desired result.

Always err on the side of slightly undercooking your pasta because it will finish cooking in the sauce, which is one of the reasons I always toss pasta and sauce together just before serving. The other is that it's the only way to fully integrate the two. In fact, it's worth practicing the skill of tossing pasta and sauce in a wide sauté pan; you'll be amazed at how much it improves the finished dish.

Risotto

The thing to understand about risotto, the fact from which all other truths follow, is that it takes a long time to cook. There's a scientific reason for this: The relatively slow cooking in small amounts of gradually replenished hot liquid releases the rice's starch, which is what binds the risotto together.

This means several things. (1) You need to have about 30 minutes available to stand over the stove and stir, and stir, and stir; do not plan to do other things while making risotto. (2) You need a heavy-bottomed pot because the rice will be in there a long time and you'll likely scorch it if you don't protect it properly. (3) Don't get cute and try to pour in more stock than you're supposed to at a time or crank the heat to get the rice to absorb it more quickly. It won't work. Take the time and the risotto will pay you back with flavor and texture that's worth every second of patient stirring.

Since this book promises the convenience of make-ahead cooking, I'll share the best risotto tip I know for the home kitchen. Contrary to popular belief, you can make risotto in advance. Here's what you do: Cook the risotto up to the point where you would add the last addition of stock. Transfer the risotto to a baking sheet, and spread it out so it can cool as quickly as possible. Then transfer it to an airtight container and refrigerate it for up to 6 hours or overnight. To finish the risotto, reheat it in a pot set over low heat while you bring the last addition of stock to a simmer in a separate pot. Stir the stock into the risotto and finish with any meats or vegetables, which you can also precook, cool, and reheat in the same manner.

Note that these pasta and risotto recipes also offer versatility in menu planning. Pasta and risotto are classically served as an early course in Italian meals, but the ones in this chapter are intended as main-course affairs. That said, you can also serve smaller portions as appetizers, or use them in a uniquely American way as side dishes to meats, fish, poultry, and game.

Stews

Like chili, stews are highly adaptable to personal taste and you should feel free to vary the ingredients in the recipes that follow, altering the meats, vegetables, herbs, and cooking liquids. As with the other recipes in this book, I've given variations following the individual recipes. But in the case of these stews, you're on fairly safe ground if you deviate further afield, creating your own house versions that, due largely to this ease of adaptability, epitomize home cooking.

Root Vegetable Stew with Cumin, Coriander, and Millet

■ *Serves 6* ■

I devised this tangy, chunky stew with vegetarians in mind, but it's not only for them; in fact, it should satisfy even the most voracious carnivore. I know this because I'm just a notch away from caveman-ship myself and it hits me just right. What it lacks in protein it makes up for with tantalizing spices such as cumin and coriander.

You might not be familiar with millet because it isn't well known in the United States. It is, however, almost as common as rice in Africa and Asia. And—guess what?—millet is available in your local supermarket. I promise. Head for the rice and grains section, find the more unusual grains like couscous, and look left, right, up, and down. Somewhere in there you'll find millet. Buy a big bag because you're going to love what it adds to recipes: a pleasing bite that's just shy of a crunch, and a bit of starch that subtly thickens the liquid in which it's cooked. If you like, you can use barley (page 207) in its place but, because it takes longer to cook than millet, add it with the other ingredients in Step four.

This is an adaptation-friendly affair; vary the vegetables or add others to emphasize your personal favorites. Those that would work especially well are celery root, parsley root, and if you have a fondness for anise, fennel.

Serve this with Cheese Croutons (page 233).

5 plum tomatoes, cut lengthwise into
    6 pieces each
Coarse salt
Freshly ground black pepper
½ cup olive oil
1 large carrot, peeled and cut on the
    bias into 2-inch pieces
4 small turnips, peeled and quartered

2 medium parsnips, peeled and cut on
    the bias into thirds
1 small Spanish onion, peeled and cut
    into 8 wedges
4 cloves garlic, peeled and sliced
¼ cup tomato paste
1 tablespoon chopped fresh thyme
½ cup dry white wine

2 tablespoons distilled white vinegar
   (page 246)
2 teaspoons sherry vinegar
1 bay leaf, preferably fresh
4 teaspoons ground cumin
2 teaspoons ground coriander

½ teaspoon crushed red pepper
1½ quarts store-bought, reduced-
   sodium vegetable broth or
   homemade Vegetable Stock
   (page 244)
1 cup millet (page 209)

1. Thirty minutes before you want to cook, put the tomatoes in a bowl and season with salt and pepper. Set aside.

2. Heat the olive oil in a wide, deep, heavy-bottomed pot over medium-high heat until hot but not smoking. Add the carrot, turnips, parsnips, onion, and garlic and season with salt and pepper. Cook, stirring to prevent scorching, until nicely caramelized, about 15 minutes.

3. Add the tomato paste and stir for 2 minutes to coat the vegetables. Add the tomatoes and thyme and cook for 3 or 4 minutes longer.

4. Add the wine, white vinegar, and sherry vinegar, bring to a boil, and cook until nearly all of the liquid has evaporated. Add the bay leaf, cumin, coriander, and crushed red pepper. Stir in the vegetable broth and 5 teaspoons salt. Bring the liquid to a boil over high heat, then lower the heat and simmer, uncovered, for 15 minutes.

5. Add the millet, bring to a boil over high heat, then lower the heat and simmer for 30 minutes, or until the vegetables are soft and the millet is tender but still a bit al dente. If not serving immediately, let cool, cover, and refrigerate for a few days or freeze for up to 1 month. Reheat before proceeding.

6. To serve, ladle some stew into each of 6 warm bowls.

Mushroom Stew

■ *Serves 6* ■

Thanks to their meaty texture, mushrooms are often employed as a stand-in for beef, as in mushroom "burgers" and "steaks." This gave me the idea to make a mushroom stew that hits all the same flavor buttons as one made with beef. I originally conceived this recipe with portobello mushrooms in mind, but it turns out that plain ol' white mushrooms stand up better to the high heat and relatively long cooking process. The two keys to this recipe are browning the mushrooms until nicely charred (they'll leave flavorful bits in the pot just as beef does when seared), and letting the soup stand for half an hour before serving it. Without that infusing time, the mushroom flavor won't truly permeate the entire concoction.

I recommend serving this with Herbed Croutons (page 232) half immersed in the stew, leaning against the side of the bowl.

¼ cup olive oil

2 tablespoons unsalted butter

1½ pounds white mushrooms, stems removed

Coarse salt

Freshly ground black pepper

3 stalks celery, cut crosswise into ½-inch pieces

3 large carrots, peeled and cut into 1-inch pieces

1 large Spanish onion, peeled and cut into 8 wedges

1 cup dried porcini mushrooms (page 243), rinsed and crumbled

2 tablespoons all-purpose flour

1½ cups red wine

2 quarts store-bought, reduced-sodium vegetable broth or homemade Vegetable Stock (page 244)

5 canned Italian plum tomatoes, drained of excess juice then crushed by hand

5 sprigs thyme

2 bay leaves

2 tablespoons chopped fresh flat-leaf parsley leaves

1. In a large, heavy-bottomed pot, heat 2 tablespoons of the olive oil and 1 tablespoon of the butter over high heat. Add the white mushrooms, season with salt and pepper, and cook until well browned, or even slightly charred, about 5 minutes per side. Transfer the mushrooms to a bowl using tongs or a slotted spoon and set aside.

2. Add the remaining 2 tablespoons olive oil and 1 tablespoon butter to the pot and melt the butter over medium-high heat. Add the celery, carrots, onion, and porcini, season with salt and pepper, and cook, stirring, until softened and lightly browned, about 8 minutes. Sprinkle the flour over the vegetables and stir for 2 to 3 minutes, to coat them well. It's okay if the flour browns a bit.

3. Add the red wine and bring to a boil, stirring to scrape up any bits of mushroom or flour stuck to the bottom of the pot. Cook until the wine has almost completely evaporated, about 4 minutes.

4. Add the broth, tomatoes, thyme, and bay leaves and stir. Taste and adjust the seasoning if necessary. Bring the liquid to a boil, then lower the heat and simmer, uncovered, until the vegetables are softened but still hold their shape, about 35 minutes.

5. Return the mushrooms to the pot along with any liquid they have given off while resting. Bring to a boil over high heat, and boil for 8 minutes. Turn off the heat and let the stew rest, uncovered, for 30 minutes. If not serving immediately, let cool, cover, and refrigerate for a few days or freeze for up to 1 month.

6. To serve, gently reheat the stew. Stir in the parsley, remove and discard the bay leaves and thyme sprigs, and ladle some stew into each of 6 bowls.

VARIATION

To make this stew into an even more substantial main course, add precooked and cooled egg noodles or pastina (page 217). One-quarter pound pasta will be plenty when cooked.

Butternut Squash and
Wild Mushroom Risotto

■ Serves 6 ■

Risotto is the Leonard Zelig of Italian gastronomy—a dish that takes on the character of whatever you stir into it. (Leonard Zelig is the Woody Allen character in the film of the same name who took on the physical traits of whomever he came into contact with. If you're never seen it, rent it.)

This risotto is perfect for the fall because it makes the most of two seasonal stalwarts—butternut squash and wild mushrooms—sautéing each separately and then seasoning them with the herbs that suit them best. The result is a sumptuous vegetarian main course. I also recommended it as a side dish to Florentine Pot Roast with Red Wine, Mushrooms, and Tomatoes (page 178) or Mushroom-Braised Short Ribs (page 174). The supporting flavors are so alluring that this would also be delicious made with white mushrooms.

See page 76 for a great make-ahead risotto tip.

12 tablespoons (1½ sticks) unsalted butter

1 large butternut squash (about 2 pounds) peeled, halved lengthwise, seeds discarded, and cut into ½-inch dice

Coarse salt

Freshly ground black pepper

2 tablespoons chopped fresh marjoram or sage leaves

1 clove garlic, peeled and minced

1 pound assorted wild mushrooms (preferably a mix of 3, such as chanterelle, cremini, and shiitake), each type kept separate and cut into small dice

2 tablespoons chopped fresh thyme leaves

2 quarts store-bought, reduced-sodium chicken or vegetable broth, or homemade Chicken or Vegetable Stock (page 244)

2 tablespoons olive oil

1 large Spanish onion, peeled and cut into small dice

1 pound (2 cups) arborio rice

1 cup dry white wine

1. Melt 2 tablespoons of the butter in a large, heavy-bottomed pot over medium-high heat. Add the squash cubes, season with salt and pepper, and cook, stirring, until browned and slightly softened but still holding their shape, about 12 minutes. Transfer the squash to a bowl, season with the marjoram, and set aside.

2. Wipe out the pot, return it to the stove, add another 2 tablespoons of the butter and a pinch of the minced garlic and cook over medium-high heat until the butter has melted. Add one type of mushroom (or if using just 1 kind, add one-third) and sauté until lightly browned, fragrant, and softened, 5 to 7 minutes based on the type. Transfer the mushrooms to a bowl. Repeat twice with the remaining mushrooms and garlic, using 2 tablespoons of butter each time. Once all of the mushrooms have been cooked and scraped into the bowl, stir in the thyme and set aside. If not making the risotto immediately, you can cool and refrigerate the squash and mushrooms in separate containers overnight. Let them come to room temperature before making the risotto; they will reheat when they are stirred in at the end.

3. Pour the broth into a pot and bring to a simmer over low heat.

4. Wipe out the mushroom pot once more, put over medium-high heat, and add the olive oil and 2 more tablespoons of the butter. Add the onion and cook until softened but not browned, about 4 minutes. Add the rice, stir to coat it with the butter and oil, and cook for about 4 minutes. Add the wine, bring to a boil, and cook, stirring, until it evaporates nearly completely.

5. Ladle 1 cup of simmering broth into the rice and cook, stirring, until it is nearly absorbed. Continue to add broth in ½-cup increments, stirring the rice constantly. When you are down to the last 2 cups or so, add the broth in smaller increments until the rice is softened but still a bit al dente. (You may not need all of the broth, or you may need to supplement it with more broth or water.) This step should take about 18 minutes altogether.

6. To serve, stir in the reserved mushrooms and squash and remaining 2 tablespoons butter. Season with salt and pepper and divide the risotto among 6 warm bowls.

Butternut Squash and Wild Mushroom Risotto Cakes

For a side dish, cool any leftover risotto and refrigerate in an airtight container overnight. (Use it the next day or the vegetables will become unappealingly mushy.) Form the risotto into 1-inch-thick discs. Spread some all-purpose flour out on a plate and press the cakes into the flour to coat. Warm ¼ cup olive oil in a wide, deep sauté pan over medium-high heat. Fry the risotto cakes until golden brown, about 3 minutes per side, and serve immediately.

Shrimp, Lemon, and Tarragon Risotto

■ *Serves 6* ■

Many people consider risotto too heavy to eat in summer, but you can serve this version, featuring shrimp and lightened up with lots of lemon, on the hottest day of the year and it would refresh. The amount of lemon juice and zest will depend on the freshness and intensity of the lemons, so add in small increments, tasting as you go.

2 quarts store-bought, reduced-sodium vegetable or chicken broth, or homemade Vegetable or Chicken Stock (page 244)

18 large shrimp, peeled, deveined, and butterflied (see note, page 87)

2 tablespoons olive oil

4 tablespoons unsalted butter

1 large Spanish onion, peeled and cut into small dice

1 pound arborio rice (2 cups)

1 cup dry white wine

About 2 tablespoons grated lemon zest

About 2 tablespoons fresh lemon juice

2 tablespoons chopped fresh tarragon leaves

Coarse salt

Freshly ground black pepper

1. Pour the broth into a pot large enough to hold the shrimp and bring to a boil over high heat. Add the shrimp and poach at a simmer, lowering the heat if needed, until firm and pink, about 5 minutes. Remove the shrimp with a slotted spoon and set them aside on a plate. Keep the broth simmering over low heat.

2. Heat the olive oil and melt 2 tablespoons of the butter in a large, heavy-bottomed pot over medium-high heat until hot but not smoking. Add the onion and cook until softened but not browned, about 4 minutes. Add the rice, stir to coat well, and cook for about 4 minutes. Add the wine, bring to a boil, and cook, stirring, until nearly all of the wine has evaporated.

3. Ladle 1 cup of simmering broth into the rice and cook, stirring, until it is nearly absorbed. Continue to add broth in ½-cup increments, stirring the rice constantly.

When you are down to the last 2 cups or so, add the broth in smaller increments until the rice is softened but still a bit al dente. (You may not need all of the broth, or you may need to supplement it with more broth or water.) This step should take about 18 minutes altogether.

4. Stir in 1 tablespoon lemon zest and 1 tablespoon lemon juice. Taste and adjust with additional zest or juice as needed until the risotto attains a nice, bright flavor. Stir in the reserved shrimp, the tarragon, and the remaining 2 tablespoons butter. Season with salt and pepper.

5. To serve, divide the risotto among 6 warm dinner plates or shallow bowls.

VARIATION

Bay Scallop, Lemon, and Tarragon Risotto

This dish would be equally delicious with delicate little bay scallops. Simply replace the shrimp with an equal quantity of scallops.

TOMORROW'S TABLE

If you plan on leftovers (perhaps you're only cooking for 2), leave out the lemon and make a fritatta (an Italian omelet) using the leftover risotto for breakfast the next day: Preheat the broiler and heat 2 tablespoons olive oil in a wide, deep, ovenproof sauté pan over medium-high heat. Add the leftover risotto to the pan, spreading it out with a spatula. As the risotto warms, break 3 eggs into a bowl and season with salt and pepper. Beat the eggs and pour them over the risotto in the pan, using the spatula to gently lift the risotto and let the eggs seep under it. When the eggs begin to set, transfer the pan to the oven and broil until puffy and lightly golden on top. Cut into wedges and serve at once.

WHY BUTTERFLY?

When scoring the back of a shrimp's tail to get at and remove the vein, a little extra pressure on the knife will deepen the cut and make the tail flare out. This is referred to as "butterflying" the shrimp. I butterfly shrimp because it ensures the entire tail has a uniform thickness, causing it to cook more quickly and evenly. Be careful not to cut all the way through the shrimp when butterflying.

Baked Gnocchi Carbonara

■ *Serves 8* ■

Pasta carbonara's soul is bacon, butter, cheese, and egg, so you know it's gotta be delicious. The recipe allows for interpretation, but the essentials are pasta, crisped bacon dice, grated cheese, and raw eggs that cook on contact with the hot pasta. This is an even more decadent version of pasta carbonara made with gnocchi, the small potato dumplings, and baked in the oven. In addition to this dish, the recipe for gnocchi is a valuable one to add to your repertoire. The key to its success is not overworking the dough, so stop kneading or shaping it as soon as you've completed each step. (You can also save a step by purchasing gnocchi from the dried-pasta section or refrigerator-freezer case in your market.)

1½ pounds baking potatoes (about 2 medium potatoes)
Coarse salt
1¾ cups all-purpose flour, plus more for dusting
3 large eggs, at room temperature
½ pound slab bacon (page 241), cut into ¼-inch strips

4 tablespoons unsalted butter
1 cup freshly grated Parmesan cheese
½ cup freshly grated Pecorino Romano cheese
Freshly ground black pepper
½ cup dried bread crumbs

1. Put the potatoes in a large, heavy-bottomed pot and cover with cold water by 2 inches. Salt the water, bring to a boil over high heat, and cook until the potatoes are done, about 20 minutes. (A sharp, thin-bladed knife will pierce easily to their center.) While the potatoes are cooking, break 1 of the eggs into a small bowl and beat it with a whisk.

2. Drain the potatoes and, when cool enough to handle, peel them. Pass them through a ricer, or transfer them to a large bowl and mash them with a masher, but don't overwork them.

3. Lightly dust a clean, dry work surface with a little flour and turn the warm pota-

toes out onto it. Sprinkle the remaining flour over the potatoes and knead together just until combined. Make a well in the center of the dough and pour the beaten egg into it. Use a fork to work the egg into the dough. Once combined, knead the dough by hand until it is uniformly smooth and not at all sticky, about 2 minutes.

4. Divide the dough into 6 equal portions and roll each portion out into a rope, about ½ inch in diameter. Cut each rope into 1-inch segments and roll each piece into a small ball. If not serving immediately, place the gnocchi on a baking sheet and freeze until hardened, 3 to 4 hours. Transfer to a plastic bag and store in the freezer until ready to cook, or for up to 1 month.

5. Bring a pot of salted water to a boil over high heat. Fill a large bowl halfway with ice water and line a baking sheet with a clean kitchen towel. Add the gnocchi to the pot and cook until they rise to the surface, about 3 minutes for fresh or 5 minutes for frozen. Use a slotted spoon to transfer the gnocchi to the ice water to cool them, and then transfer them to the prepared baking sheet. Pat the tops of the gnocchi dry with paper towels and set aside.

6. Preheat the broiler and set a large casserole in the oven to warm it. Break the remaining 2 eggs into a bowl, season them with salt and pepper, and beat them with a whisk.

7. Put the bacon in the casserole and set under the broiler until the bacon is browned and crispy, about 5 minutes. Remove the casserole from the oven, add the gnocchi, butter, ½ cup of the Parmesan, and the Pecorino. Season with pepper. Stir gently for 1 minute to incorporate the ingredients, being careful not to break the gnocchi. Return the casserole to the oven and cook just long enough to heat the gnocchi, about 2 minutes. Remove the casserole from the oven, and add the eggs, stirring gently for 1 minute to incorporate. They should start to cook on contact with the gnocchi.

8. Remove the casserole from the oven. Top the gnocchi with the remaining Parmesan and the bread crumbs and broil in the oven until the cheese is lightly browned, about 1 minute. Serve the casserole family style from the center of the table.

Macaroni and Goat Cheese

■ *Serves 8* ■

Is it just me, or do people take macaroni and cheese for granted? I think the lack of appreciation began with those prepackaged macaroni kits in which low-grade pasta comes in one bag and an unidentifiable cheese goop or powder in another. This recipe is my attempt to illustrate a simple truth: If you approach macaroni and cheese with the same care that you do other pasta dishes, making a thoughtful decision about the pasta and the cheese, it is pretty special. Here, I recommend a small pasta such as tubetti or tubettini (page 217), though you might opt for the kitsch value of elbow macaroni. Use a fresh, creamy goat cheese that you know and love or, if you don't have one, you will in all likelihood do just fine with an inexpensive vacuum-sealed one.

This recipe includes a béchamel—a creamy sauce of egg, butter, flour, cheese, and milk—which is used in a number of classic pasta recipes, especially lasagna. Usually it's made with milk that's been preheated in a separate pot, but I find that by allowing the milk to make contact with the bottom of the pot before whisking with the other ingredients, this is not necessary.

1 large egg yolk
4 tablespoons unsalted butter
½ cup all-purpose flour
2 cups whole milk
½ cup freshly grated Parmesan cheese
1 pound fresh, creamy goat cheese,
    cut into small pieces

Coarse salt
Freshly ground black pepper
2 pounds tubetti or tubettini pasta,
    cooked al dente (page 217)
½ cup dried bread crumbs

1. Preheat the broiler. Break the egg into a small mixing bowl, set aside. Place an enamelware casserole in the oven to warm.

2. In a large, heavy-bottomed pot, melt the butter over medium heat. Add the flour a little at a time, whisking it into the butter to incorporate thoroughly without making lumps. Slowly drizzle in the milk, letting it come briefly into contact with the bottom of the hot pot to warm it a bit before whisking it into the mixture. Add a few tablespoons of the hot mixture to the reserved egg yolk and whisk to combine, then pour the egg yolk mixture into the pot. Whisk in the Parmesan.

3. Add three-quarters of the goat cheese, 1 piece at a time, whisking it into the sauce. Season with salt and pepper to taste. Add the pasta to the pot and stir to coat it with the sauce and warm it through.

4. Remove the casserole from the oven. Transfer the pasta mixture to the casserole. Dot the top with the remaining goat cheese, and then sprinkle with the bread crumbs. Broil until the crumbs are golden brown, 1 to 2 minutes. If not serving immediately, let cool, cover, and refrigerate for a few days or freeze for up to 1 month. Let thaw to room temperature and reheat under the broiler before serving.

5. To serve, present the casserole family style from the center of the table.

VARIATIONS

Macaroni with Goat Cheese and Roasted Mushrooms

Balance the tangy, creamy goat cheese with the earthy, slightly nutty flavor of roasted mushrooms: Roast some wild mushrooms (page 33), chop them, and add them to the pot along with the pasta in Step 3.

Macaroni with Vermont Cheddar

For a sharper flavor, closer to the macaroni you probably remember from childhood, replace the goat cheese with white Vermont cheddar cheese.

Two-Cheese Macaroni

For a gooey delight, eliminate the goat cheese and increase the Parmesan to 3 cups, using it all in Step 3. Omit the bread crumbs, and top the pasta with ½ cup shredded mozzarella before passing under the broiler. Finish with a sprinkling of chopped basil leaves just before serving.

Tubetti with White Wine and Clams

■ Serves 6 ■

I demonstrated this recipe on the morning program *Live! with Regis and Kelly* as part of a series in which Italian-American chefs cooked recipes from their childhood. It features many of my all-time-favorites ingredients, like Great Northern beans and sweet sausage, and is remarkably easy to cook. Just line them all up and add them to the pot one after the other, which for me is a culinary trip down memory lane. This simplicity made for a fail-safe television appearance and doesn't hurt at home, either.

2 tablespoons olive oil

8 ounces sweet sausage (about 2 small links), casing removed and meat crumbled

4 cloves garlic, peeled and sliced

24 small clams, cleaned and scrubbed (page 49)

½ cup dry white wine

2½ cups store-bought, reduced-sodium chicken broth or homemade Chicken Stock (page 244)

1 cup cooked tubetti pasta (from about ¼ cup dried, page 217)

1½ cups canned Great Northern white beans, drained and rinsed

1 teaspoon crushed red pepper

½ cup freshly grated Parmesan cheese

2 tablespoons chopped fresh flat-leaf parsley leaves

2 tablespoons chopped fresh basil leaves

Extra-virgin olive oil, optional

1. Heat the oil in a large, shallow pot until quite hot. Add the sausage and brown it nicely for 2 to 3 minutes, adding the garlic after 1 minute. Add the clams and wine, cover the pot, and cook for 2 to 3 minutes or until the clams pop open. Discard any clams that have not opened.

2. Add the chicken broth and bring to a boil. Add the pasta and beans and let them heat through for 1 or 2 minutes. Add the crushed red pepper and Parmesan, stir, and cook for 2 to 3 minutes. Stir in the parsley and basil before removing from the heat.

3. To serve, ladle some pasta and sauce into each of 6 warm bowls and drizzle with extra-virgin olive oil, if desired.

Spaghetti with Tuna and Tomato

Canned tuna and tomato may seem an unlikely pairing, but they are actually a time-honed combo in Italian kitchens and make up one of the pasta sauces I loved most as a child. If you've only had canned American tuna, seek out the Italian or Spanish tuna specified in this recipe. Often packed in glass jars, its fresh tuna flavor, enriched by the oil, elevates this product to a true delicacy that should be found a shelf above domestic canned tuna, if there were any justice in the world of supermarket placement. If you have a fondness for the salty quality of this dish, you can punch it up with the addition of capers and chopped anchovy fillets.

2 tablespoons olive oil
1 small Spanish onion, peeled and
    cut into small dice
1 clove garlic, peeled and minced
One 12-ounce jar imported Italian
    or Spanish preserved tuna packed
    in oil, drained
1 pound dried spaghetti

One 35-ounce can whole imported
    tomatoes in their liquid, crushed
    by hand
Coarse salt
Freshly ground black pepper
2 tablespoons chopped fresh flat-leaf
    parsley leaves

1. Bring a large pot of salted water to a boil over high heat.

2. Meanwhile, heat the olive oil in a wide, deep-sided sauté pan over medium-high heat until hot but not smoking. Add the onion and garlic and cook, stirring, for 3 minutes without browning them. Add the tuna and cook for 5 minutes.

3. Add the spaghetti to the boiling water and cook until al dente, about 9 minutes.

4. While the spaghetti is cooking, add the tomatoes to the tuna, stir, season with salt and pepper, and simmer over medium heat.

5. When the spaghetti is done, drain it and transfer it to the tomato sauce. Add the parsley and toss well.

6. To serve, ladle some pasta and sauce into each of 6 warm bowls.

Tuna Noodle Casserole

■ *Serves 6* ■

Tuna noodle casserole is a classic of American home cooking, in part because it requires little more than a can of tuna, a pound of pasta, and cream of mushroom soup. This recipe ups the ante with high-quality imported tuna (see page 93 for more about this) and a rich, homemade béchamel sauce. Rather than the classic egg noodle, this casserole uses pennette, small tubular pasta (discussed on page 217). It's usually used in soups, but I like it here because it's smaller than the pieces of tuna, and its centers fill up with cream, so flavors and textures other than pasta dominate.

1 large egg
6 tablespoons unsalted butter
½ cup plus 2 tablespoons all-purpose
    flour
3 cups whole milk
Coarse salt
Freshly ground black pepper
¾ cup freshly grated Parmesan cheese
1 pound pennette pasta, cooked
    al dente and drained (page 217)

One 12-ounce can imported Italian or
    Spanish preserved tuna packed in
    oil, drained
2 cloves garlic, peeled and minced
2 tablespoons fresh oregano leaves, or
    1 tablespoon dried oregano
2 tablespoons minced fresh flat-leaf
    parsley leaves
½ cup dried bread crumbs

1. Preheat the broiler. Put the egg yolk in a small bowl; set aside. Place an enamelware casserole in the oven to warm.

2. In a large, heavy-bottomed pot, melt the butter over medium heat. Add the flour a little at a time, whisking it into the butter to incorporate thoroughly without making lumps. Slowly drizzle in the milk, letting it come briefly into contact with the bottom of the hot pot to warm it a bit before whisking it into the mixture. Add a few tablespoons of the hot mixture to the reserved egg yolk and whisk to combine, then pour the egg yolk mixture into the pot. Whisk in the Parmesan.

3. Add the pasta, tuna, garlic, oregano, and parsley to the pot and stir to integrate the flavors. Remove the casserole from the oven. Transfer the pasta mixture to the casserole. Top with the bread crumbs and broil until the bread crumbs are golden brown, 1 to 2 minutes. If not serving immediately, let cool, cover, and refrigerate for a few days or freeze for up to 1 month. Let thaw to room temperature and reheat under the broiler before serving.

4. To serve, present the casserole family style from the center of the table.

Manhattan-Style Fish Stew

Serves 6

This stew is inspired by the foundation of bacon and tomato in a Manhattan clam chowder, but rather than shellfish it uses cod to produce a thick and hearty stew. A simple recipe, it calls for adding many ingredients in quick succession, so take the time to have them ready and arranged in the order in which you will use them before you put the pot to the fire.

5 plum tomatoes, diced
Coarse salt
Freshly ground black pepper
2½ pounds skinless cod fillet, cut into 1-inch dice
2 tablespoons olive oil
Garlic powder
2 tablespoons chopped fresh flat-leaf parsley leaves
½ pound slab bacon (page 241), diced (about 2 cups)
1 large carrot, peeled and cut into small dice
1 large Spanish onion, peeled and cut into small dice

2 stalks celery, peeled and cut into small dice
3 cloves garlic, peeled and minced
3 tablespoons tomato paste
Pinch of sugar
Pinch of crushed red pepper
½ cup dry white wine
½ teaspoon distilled white vinegar (page 246)
3 cups water
Two 8-ounce bottles clam juice
Pinch of saffron threads (page 55)
2 medium baking potatoes, peeled and cut into small dice

1. Thirty minutes before you want to cook, put the tomatoes in a bowl and season with salt and pepper. Put the cod cubes in another bowl, drizzle with the olive oil, and season with salt, pepper, garlic powder, and the parsley. Set aside.

2. In a large, heavy-bottomed, ovenproof pot, cook the bacon over medium-high heat until it turns golden brown and gives off enough fat to coat the bottom of the pot, about 7 minutes.

3. Add the carrot, onion, celery, and garlic. Season with salt and pepper and cook, stirring, for 3 to 4 minutes, until slightly softened. Add the tomato paste and sugar and stir to coat the other ingredients. Cook for 2 to 3 minutes. Add the reserved tomatoes, crushed red pepper, wine, and vinegar, bring to a boil, and cook for 5 minutes. Add the water, clam juice, saffron, and the potatoes. Bring the liquid to a boil over high heat, and then lower the heat and simmer for 20 minutes. Add 2 tablespoons salt and ½ teaspoon black pepper and simmer for another 10 minutes until the potatoes are cooked almost all the way through to the center. (Remove and cut into one to check if you're not sure.) If not serving immediately, let cool, cover, and refrigerate for a few days or freeze for up to 1 month. Reheat gently when ready to proceed.

4. Lower the heat so that the soup barely simmers and add the reserved fish. Cook just until the cod is heated through, about 5 minutes.

5. To serve, ladle some soup into each of 6 warm bowls, making sure to include a good mix of fish and potatoes in each serving.

VARIATION

Mediterranean Fish Stew

Use ¾ pound each of boneless, skinless cod, swordfish, and mackerel for a greater range of flavor and texture. To hammer home the theme, add ½ cup pitted, slivered, green olives and 1 tablespoon capers, rinsed and drained. Serve this variation with Aïoli Croutons (page 230).

Clam Chowder

Since this recipe is based on classic clam chowder, you can make clam chowder by omitting the cod and bottled clam juice and replacing them with 3 pounds small clams, rinsed and scrubbed (page 49). Cook the clams with wine and garlic according to the instructions for steaming the mussels in the Mussel Chowder (page 51), Step 2. Strain and reserve their cooking liquid, and remove and discard the shells. Then, replace the clam juice in Step 3 of the above recipe with the reserved cooking liquid. In Step 4, add the shelled clams in place of the fish cubes.

Roasted Fish and Shellfish with Tomatoes and Parsley

Serves 6

This recipe was going to be a take on a Tuscan dish called *tegamone,* which is a hodge-podge of fish and shellfish that's started on the stovetop with tomato and white wine, then baked in the oven. But I got carried away and ended up with this cross section of tasty marine life united by a light, tomato-wine-saffron cooking liquid and rounded out with pastina (page 217). The recipe is also noteworthy because it simultaneously poaches and roasts the ingredients by placing their cooking vessel in the hot confines of an oven. (I use a similar technique to braise lamb shanks, page 167.)

Just to let you know, starting at about Step five, this recipe gets pretty specific about where and how to add the seafood to the pot. It's a bit unusual, but not difficult, and essential to getting everything to finish cooking at the same time. To make it as easy as possible to put the individual ingredients in the right place, select the widest pot you have so that you can get everything in there without trouble.

6 plum tomatoes, cut into small dice
Coarse salt
Freshly ground black pepper
Sugar
2 tablespoons olive oil
1 large Spanish onion, peeled and
    minced
3 cloves garlic, peeled and minced
2 tablespoons tomato paste
2 cups dry white wine
1 quart store-bought, reduced-sodium
    chicken broth or homemade
    Chicken Stock (page 244)
Pinch of saffron threads (page 55)

1 cup pastina (page 217), couscous
    (page 208), or millet (page 209)
12 small clams, cleaned and scrubbed
    (page 49)
12 mussels, scrubbed and debearded
    (page 53)
6 large scallops
20 ounces 1-inch-thick skinless swordfish
    steak, cut into 1-inch cubes
8 medium shrimp, preferably head on,
    shelled, deveined, and butterflied
    (page 87)
2 tablespoons chopped fresh flat-leaf
    parsley leaves

1. Thirty minutes before you want to cook, put the tomatoes in a bowl and season with salt, pepper, and a pinch of sugar. Set aside.

2. Preheat the oven to 450°F.

3. Heat the olive oil in a wide, deep, ovenproof pot over medium-high heat until hot but not smoking. Add the onion and garlic and sauté until softened but not browned. Add the reserved tomato and tomato paste and cook, stirring, until the ingredients are well incorporated, a few minutes more.

4. Add the wine, bring to a boil, and cook, scraping up any bits stuck onto the bottom of the pot, until the wine is reduced by half. Add the chicken broth and saffron, bring the liquid to a boil over high heat, then reduce the heat so that the liquid simmers. Taste and adjust the seasoning if necessary.

5. Add the pastina, scattering it evenly over the pot, and let it settle to the bottom. If using millet, let it cook for 15 minutes before proceeding.

6. Add the clams and mussels to the pot, confining them to one side, and carefully immerse them in the liquid. Season the scallops and swordfish with salt and pepper and carefully add them to the other side of the pot. Place the shrimp on top of the scallops and swordfish, pushing them just under the surface of the liquid.

7. Transfer the pot to the oven and roast for 7 or 8 minutes. Use tongs or a kitchen spoon to carefully turn over the mussels and clams. Cook for another 7 or 8 minutes until the scallops and shrimp are nicely plumped.

8. Remove the pot from the oven. If the shellfish haven't popped open, use a slotted spoon to transfer the scallops, swordfish, and shrimp to a plate and cover with aluminum foil to keep warm. Cover the pot and place over medium heat for 2 to 3 minutes, or until the shellfish, or most of them, have popped open. Discard any shellfish that have not opened by this point.

9. To serve, use a slotted spoon to distribute the fish, scallops, and pasta among individual bowls. Ladle the broth on top and sprinkle each serving with the parsley.

Sautéed Calamari with
White Wine, Garlic, and Clam Broth

Serves 6

Contrary to popular belief, calamari (aka squid) don't come out of the ocean already cut into rings, coated with bread crumbs, fried, and accompanied by a thimble of marinara sauce for dipping. They actually come fully intact and are usually available cleaned, leaving you little more to do than slice them. There are a number of ways to enjoy calamari, but this is one of my favorites: in a white sauce of wine, garlic, and clam juice that underscores the calamari's gentle flavor. In this context, the bacon is especially important: It anchors the dish with a salty, smoky undercurrent.

Serve this over pasta such as spaghetti (page 218), linguine (page 219), or capellini (page 216), or with a slice of toasted Italian bread.

4 ounces slab bacon (page 241), diced (about 1 cup)

2 ounces Genoa salami, finely sliced (about ½ cup)

1 medium carrot, peeled and cut into small dice

1 medium Spanish onion, peeled and cut into small dice

4 cloves garlic, peeled and thinly sliced, plus 3 cloves garlic, peeled and minced

2 tablespoons tomato paste

Pinch of sugar

1 cup dry white wine

1 tablespoon distilled white vinegar (page 246)

One 28-ounce can Italian plum tomatoes, drained of liquid and crushed by hand

Two 8-ounce bottles clam juice

½ teaspoon crushed red pepper

Coarse salt

Freshly ground black pepper

1 tablespoon chopped fresh oregano leaves

1 bay leaf

3 tablespoons olive oil

4 pounds squid, tentacles removed and discarded or saved for another use, bodies split open lengthwise and cut into ¼-inch strips

1. In a heavy-bottomed pot, cook the bacon and salami over medium-high heat until crisp and they have rendered enough fat to coat the bottom of the pot, about 5 minutes.

2. Add the carrot, onion, and sliced garlic and cook, stirring, until the vegetables are tender but not at all browned, 7 to 8 minutes.

3. Add the tomato paste and sugar and stir to coat the other ingredients. Add the wine and the vinegar and continue cooking for 2 minutes. Stir in the tomatoes, clam juice, and crushed red pepper. Season with salt and pepper if necessary. Bring to a boil over high heat, and then lower the heat so the liquid simmers. Add the oregano and bay leaf and simmer for 25 minutes.

4. Heat the oil in large skillet over medium-high heat until very hot but not smoking. Season the squid with salt and pepper. Add the minced garlic and squid to the skillet and cook until the squid just begin to curl, 1 to 2 minutes. Add the tomato sauce to the pan and toss well. Discard the bay leaf.

5. To serve, divide the squid and sauce among 6 warm bowls bowls.

VARIATIONS

Shrimp with White Wine, Garlic, and Clam Broth

Peeled, deveined, and butterflied shrimp (page 87) make a fine alternative to the squid here. Rather than sautéing them, omit Step 4, season the shrimp with salt and pepper, and poach them in the sauce at a gentle simmer for 1 to 2 minutes after completing Step 3.

Shrimp Stew with Leeks

Serves 6

Two words: simple elegance. Leeks are so often combined with other vegetables in soups or stocks that it's easy to forget how delicious they are on their own or when paired with one perfect companion, in this case shrimp. This dish focuses on the leek's gentle onion flavor and reminds you, once and for all, not to take this beautiful, pale green staple for granted.

8 tablespoons (1 stick) unsalted
    butter
3 cloves garlic, peeled and minced
4 medium leeks, white parts plus
    ½ inch of green, outer leaves
    discarded, cut on the bias into
    ½-inch pieces, well washed, and
    dried
1 cup dry white wine

2 cups store-bought, reduced-sodium
    chicken broth or homemade
    Chicken Stock (page 244)
Coarse salt
Freshly ground black pepper
30 large shrimp, preferably head on,
    peeled and deveined (page 87)
2 tablespoons minced fresh chives
Juice of ½ lemon

1. Melt 4 tablespoons of the butter in a heavy-bottomed pot over medium-high heat. Add the garlic and sauté for 2 minutes, taking care not to let the butter or garlic brown. Add the leeks and sauté gently until tender, about 4 minutes.

2. Stir in the white wine, bring to a boil, and cook for 2 to 3 minutes. Add the chicken broth, bring to a boil, and season with salt and pepper. Lower the heat so the liquid simmers gently, and whisk in the remaining 4 tablespoons butter. Add the shrimp and cook for 4 minutes. If the shrimp aren't totally immersed, flip them after 2 minutes and cook for another 2 minutes.

3. Divide the shrimp among 6 bowls, arranging them like the spokes of a wheel. Stir the chives and lemon juice into the broth, then spoon some broth over the shrimp in each bowl. Serve at once.

This dish is equally delicious with 40 tiny, tender bay scallops (or 20 larger sea or diver scallops, cut in half crosswise) in place of the shrimp.

Chicken Hearts and Gizzards in Italian-Style Tomato Sauce

■ Serves 8 ■

Chicken hearts and gizzards are distinctly dense and rich and this recipe—a variation of the one my grandmother made when I was a kid—is like home to me, my personal favorite comfort food. Since we enjoyed it in a number of guises, I'm giving you the same option here—use this sauce to top your favorite pasta (pages 215 to 220), polenta (page 210), or simply spoon it over toasted bread. If you're feeling particularly decadent, grill or toast bread slices spread with butter and minced garlic in a 400°F oven and dunk your way through an entire bowl.

If you think you can't find hearts and gizzards in your supermarket, guess again. You'll be surprised how close they are to the other chicken parts in your grocer's refrigerator.

⅓ cup olive oil
2 pounds chicken hearts and gizzards
Coarse salt
Freshly ground black pepper
2 medium carrots, peeled and cut into
    ½-inch dice
1 large onion, peeled and cut into
    ½-inch dice
6 cloves garlic, peeled and thinly sliced
¼ cup tomato paste

¼ cup dry white wine
5 pounds plum tomatoes, crushed
    by hand
1 cup water
¼ cup extra-virgin olive oil
2 bay leaves, crumbled
¼ cup chopped fresh basil leaves
2 tablespoons chopped fresh thyme
    leaves
Pinch of crushed red pepper

1. Heat the olive oil in a large, heavy-bottomed pot over medium-high heat. Add the hearts and gizzards, season with salt and pepper, and brown on all sides, 3 to 4 minutes. Transfer the hearts and gizzards to a plate and set aside.

2. Add the carrots, onion, and garlic to the pot and cook, stirring, until softened but not browned, about 5 minutes. Add the tomato paste, stir to coat the other ingredients, and cook for 2 to 3 minutes. Add the white wine, bring to a boil, and let reduce for 2 minutes.

3. Add the tomatoes, water, extra-virgin olive oil, bay leaves, basil, thyme, and crushed red pepper. Stir, return the hearts and gizzards to the pot, raise the heat, and bring to a boil. Season with salt and pepper, lower the heat, and simmer gently for 90 minutes until nicely thickened and richly flavored. If not serving immediately, let cool, cover, and refrigerate for a few days or freeze for up to 1 month. Reheat before proceeding.

4. Serve over toasted bread, pasta, or polenta.

VARIATION

Sweet Sausage in Italian-Style Tomato Sauce

If you just can't warm up to the idea of eating hearts and gizzards, replace them with an equal quantity of sweet sausage removed from its casing(s). Brown the sausage in batches, breaking it up with a fork or wooden spoon as it cooks.

Red-Wine-and-Tomato-Braised Duck

■ Serves 6 ■

Come autumn, this is one of the most popular dishes at Ouest, where we serve it with gnocchi (page 88), the perfect thing to soak up all its tangy sauce. At home, duck legs have other charms: They're inexpensive, lean, and tender, an irresistible trio of traits. Make this on the first cold day of the year to fully appreciate all of its restorative qualities. This is also delicious served over egg noodles (page 217) or Mashed Potatoes (page 221).

3 plum tomatoes, cut into small dice
Coarse salt
Freshly ground black pepper
2 tablespoons olive oil
8 duck legs, available from specialty shops and gourmet markets (also see Mail-Order Sources, page 247)
¼ pound slab bacon (page 241), cut into 1-inch pieces

1 medium Spanish onion, cut into ¼-inch dice
1 large carrot, sliced on a bias into ¼-inch segments
2 cups red wine
¼ cup distilled white vinegar (page 246)
⅓ cup tomato paste

1. Thirty minutes before you want to cook, put the tomatoes in a bowl and season with salt and pepper.

2. Heat the olive oil into a large, heavy-bottomed pot and warm it over low heat until hot but not smoking. Season the duck legs with salt and pepper. Add the legs to the pan, skin side down. Cook gently, spooning off and discarding the rendered fat as it accumulates. Cook until most of the fat renders, 15 to 20 minutes longer. Turn the legs over and brown them on the other side, about 4 minutes. Remove them from the pan and set aside on a plate.

3. Pour off all but a few tablespoons of fat from the pot. Add the bacon and cook over medium-low heat, stirring to brown it and render its fat, about 8 minutes. Add the reserved tomatoes, onion, carrot, red wine, and vinegar and cook, stirring, for 1 minute. Add the tomato paste and stir to coat all the ingredients.

4. Return the duck to the pot, bring the liquid to a simmer, and braise until the duck is tender and falling off the bone, about 1 hour 15 minutes. Using tongs to hold the legs, remove the meat from the bones with a knife; it should come right off. Discard the bones. If not serving immediately, let cool, cover, and refrigerate the meat and sauce for a few days or freeze for up to 1 month. Reheat before proceeding.

5. To serve, divide the duck, vegetables, and sauce among 6 warm dinner plates or shallow bowls.

White Bean Casserole with Preserved Duck

■ *Serves 6* ■

Every winter, I crave cassoulet, the classic French white bean stew that features a variety of game and sausage. But I never feel like going to the trouble of making it from scratch, which calls for preserving duck legs, and other labor-intensive steps. This casserole is by no means a true cassoulet, but it boasts many of the same flavors and textures. One of the ways it shortcuts the classic recipe is that it calls for a store-bought duck leg confit rather than asking you to make your own. Confit duck legs are available from specialty shops and gourmet markets (also see Mail-Order sources, page 247).

I recommend serving this with a salad of sturdy bitter greens (frisée or escarole) dressed simply with oil, vinegar, and minced garlic.

2 tablespoons olive oil
8 confit duck legs
8 ounces slab bacon (page 241), cut into large dice
2 small carrots, peeled, halved lengthwise, and cut on the bias into ¼-inch pieces
1 small Spanish onion, peeled and minced
4 cloves garlic, peeled and minced
Two 1-pound-13-ounce cans cannellini beans, drained and rinsed

1 cup store-bought, reduced-sodium chicken broth or homemade Chicken Stock (page 244)
1 teaspoon chopped fresh thyme leaves
1 teaspoon chopped fresh oregano leaves
Coarse salt
Freshly ground black pepper
1½ cups dried bread crumbs

1. Preheat the oven to 375°F.

2. Heat the olive oil in a large, heavy-bottomed pot over medium heat. Add the duck confit, skin side down, and cook until nicely browned and crisp, about 10 minutes. Using tongs or a slotted spoon, transfer the legs to a plate, leaving the duck fat in the pot.

3. Add the bacon dice and cook until the fat renders and the bacon is crisp, about 7 minutes. Add the carrots, onion, and garlic, and cook until tender, 5 to 6 minutes. Add the beans, broth, thyme, and oregano. Stir, and season with just a little salt and a generous amount of pepper. Cook until the beans are warmed through, 8 to 10 minutes.

4. Use a wooden spoon to smooth the beans in an even layer on the bottom of the casserole. Return the duck legs to the casserole, skin side up, and top with the bread crumbs. If not serving immediately, let cool, cover, and refrigerate for a few days or freeze for up to 1 month. Bring to room temperature before proceeding.

5. Transfer the casserole to the oven and bake for 35 to 40 minutes, or until the top is nicely browned and the liquid is bubbling around its edges.

6. To serve, divide the casserole among 6 warm plates or bowls and serve at once.

VARIATION

White Bean Casserole with Sweet Sausage and Sage

If you can't find preserved duck, use this as a vehicle for sausage (also an important cassoulet ingredient), replacing the duck legs with four 4-ounce sweet sausages. Brown them as you would the duck in Step 2, then slice crosswise in half before returning them to the pot in Step 4.

Lentil and Garlic Sausage Stew

■ Makes 8 servings ■

Save this stew for a cold fall day, when its starchy, garlicky charms are most welcome and warming. When making it, think of the mingling of broth and lentils as you would the stock and rice in risotto (page 76): You want the overall dish to be moist but not soupy, thick but not like a porridge. Use the best extra-virgin olive oil in your cupboard here; the lentils will pay you back by acting as a conduit for all of its rich flavor.

Two ingredient notes: For the sausage, seek out a *saucisson à l'ail* or garlic sausage, which looks uncooked, although it's not. (If this is difficult to find, substitute your favorite sausage or kielbasa, as long as you select a relatively soft one that resembles bologna more than salami.) As for the lentils, nothing else comes close to the sublime ones of France's Le Puy region, which are light green instead of brown, and hold their shape beautifully when cooked.

1 tablespoon olive oil
2½ pounds garlic sausage, cut on the
    bias into ½-inch pieces, casing
    removed
1 medium Spanish onion, peeled and
    cut into small dice
2 stalks celery, cut into small dice
1 large carrot, peeled and cut into
    small dice
6 cloves garlic, peeled and sliced
¼ cup extra-virgin olive oil, plus more
    for serving

One 17½-ounce package French green
    lentils
1 tablespoon chopped fresh thyme
    leaves
1 bay leaf
Coarse salt
Freshly ground black pepper
About 1½ quarts store-bought,
    reduced-sodium chicken broth
    or homemade Chicken Stock
    (page 244)

1. Heat the olive oil in a large, heavy-bottomed pot over medium-high heat. Add the sausage and brown on both sides in batches, 7 to 8 minutes per batch, transferring them to a plate as they are browned.

2. Leave the fat in the pan. Add the onion, celery, carrot, and garlic and cook, stirring, until softened but not browned, about 5 minutes. Add the extra-virgin olive oil and lentils, stir well, and then add the thyme, bay leaf, 2 tablespoons salt, and 1½ teaspoons pepper. Add just enough broth to cover, about 1 quart. Bring to a boil over high heat, then lower the heat and simmer for 10 to 15 minutes.

3. Add 2 more cups broth and return the sausage to the pot. Simmer for about 1 hour, or until the lentils are al dente and the sausage is cooked through. If not serving immediately, let cool, cover, and refrigerate for a few days or freeze for up to 1 month. Reheat before proceeding.

4. To serve, ladle some stew into each of 8 warm bowls and drizzle each serving with extra-virgin olive oil.

VARIATIONS

The lentils on their own (without the sausage) are the perfect side dish to Seven-Hour Leg of Lamb (page 170). Use the olive oil called for in Step 1 to sauté the vegetables in Step 2 instead of using the sausage fat.

Sausage and Cabbage Stew

■ Makes 6 servings ■

Like my speedy take on cassoulet (page 108), this is a stripped-down answer to *choucroûte garni,* an Alsatian winter ritual that cooks sauerkraut with odds and ends of poultry, meats, and sausages. My recipe shortens and simplifies the ingredient list, omitting some optional, traditional items like green apples and gin, and only calling for one type of meat rather than an assortment. It also uses Savoy cabbage in place of ready-made sauerkraut, and amplifies its tangy quality by adding distilled white vinegar.

3 tablespoons olive oil
Twelve 4-ounce links sweet or spicy
    pork sausage, or a combination,
    pricked with a fork
½ large Spanish onion, peeled and cut
    into 8 wedges
8 cloves garlic, peeled and cut into
    thin slivers
½ teaspoon fennel seeds

1 small head Savoy cabbage, cut into
    8 wedges
2 cups dry white wine
2 tablespoons distilled white vinegar
    (page 246)
2 quarts store-bought, reduced-sodium
    chicken broth or homemade
    Chicken Stock (page 244)
Whole-grain mustard, optional

1. Heat the olive oil in a large, heavy-bottomed pot over medium-high heat. Add the sausages and brown on all sides for 10 to 12 minutes. Remove one from the pot and cut it open to check that it is cooked all the way though to the center. The juices should run clear instead of pink and the meat should be hot all the way in the center.

2. Remove the sausages from the pot and set aside. Pour off all but 2 tablespoons fat from the pan.

3. Add the onion, garlic, and fennel seeds and cook, stirring, until the onion softens but does not brown, about 4 minutes. Add the cabbage and cook until softened, about 5 minutes.

4. Pour in the wine and vinegar, bring to a boil, and cook until nearly completely evaporated, about 5 minutes.

5. Add the broth, bring to a boil over high heat, and then lower the heat and simmer for 60 to 90 minutes, until the flavors are well integrated and the cabbage is thoroughly softened. Return the sausages to the pot for 15 minutes to heat through.

6. To serve, divide the stew among 6 warm bowls and pass mustard on the side, if desired.

Texas-Style Chili

■ *Serves 6* ■

This chili is based on accounts I've read of chili cook-offs, where cubed meat seems to be a popular, common denominator, giving the chili what strikes me as a charming authenticity reminiscent of chuck wagons and campfires . . . not that I've ever actually participated in either. The result is a chunkier stewlike dish that leaves red-meat junkies the more satisfied because of the beefy flavor, which comes through much louder and clearer than with ground meat varieties.

Serve this over brown rice (page 211).

2 pounds beef chuck, cut into 1-inch
 chunks, trimmed of fat
Coarse salt
Freshly ground black pepper
Garlic powder
Chili powder
2 tablespoons olive oil
2 large carrots, cut into small dice
1 large Spanish onion, peeled and cut
 into small dice
1 stalk celery, cut into small dice
2 bell peppers, seeded and cut into
 small dice
10 cloves garlic, peeled and minced
2 heaping tablespoons tomato paste
Pinch of sugar

2 tablespoons all-purpose flour
1 tablespoon distilled white vinegar
 (page 246)
1 quart store-bought reduced-sodium
 beef broth
4 plum tomatoes, coarsely chopped
1 teaspoon ground cumin, plus more
 to taste
1 ancho chile, seeded, stemmed, and
 minced
Two 15-ounce cans red kidney beans,
 drained and rinsed
Sour cream, grated cheddar cheese,
 Tabasco sauce, saltines, and minced
 onion, optional

1. Put the meat in a bowl and season with 1 tablespoon each of salt, pepper, garlic powder, and chili powder. Set aside.

2. Warm the oil in a large pot over medium-high heat. Add the meat and cook until browned all over, 7 to 10 minutes, then transfer it to a plate and set aside.

3. Drain off all but a few tablespoons of the liquid from the pot. Add the carrots, onion, celery, bell peppers, and garlic, season with salt and pepper, and cook, stirring, until softened but not browned, about 5 minutes. Add the tomato paste and sugar and stir to coat the vegetables.

4. Return the meat to the pot. Sprinkle the flour over the meat and stir it in, working quickly to keep it from browning.

5. Add the vinegar and stir to loosen any bits of flour or meat stuck to the bottom of the pot. Add the broth in small increments, stirring to prevent lumps. Add the tomatoes, cumin, and ancho chile and stir. Bring the liquid to a boil over high heat.

6. Cover the pot, reduce the heat so that the liquid just simmers, and cook for 1 hour. Add the beans and continue to cook until they are very tender, about 15 minutes. If not serving immediately, let cool, cover, and refrigerate for a few days or freeze for up to 1 month. Reheat before proceeding.

7. To serve, divide the chili among 6 bowls and pass garnishes at the table in individual bowls, inviting everyone to doctor his or her chili to taste.

Beer and Beef Stew

▪ Serves 8 ▪

Most people probably think of the classic beef stew as being made with red wine, but to my mind beer is a more logical complement to the flavors of caramelized onions, sweet carrots, and—most importantly—the beef itself. The result is rich, tender chunks of beef in a tangy, savory beer sauce. Feel free to experiment with different dark beers until you find the one that suits your taste; you'll find this stew works well with a great range, including lighter styles like pale ale. This would also be delicious with millet (page 209) added during the last 30 minutes of cooking.

2 tablespoons olive oil

3 pounds beef chuck, cut into 2-inch chunks, trimmed of fat

Coarse salt

Freshly ground black pepper

3 large Spanish onions, halved, peeled, and thinly sliced

2 stalks celery, cut into small dice

3 large carrots, peeled and cut into small dice, plus 3 large carrots, peeled and cut on the bias into 1-inch pieces

3 cloves garlic, smashed and peeled

1½ pounds white mushrooms, thinly sliced

2 tablespoons dried porcini mushrooms (page 243), rinsed

3 sprigs thyme

2 bay leaves

One 12-ounce bottle dark beer

About 2 cups store-bought, reduced-sodium beef broth

2 tablespoons chopped fresh flat-leaf parsley leaves

1. Heat the oil in a large, heavy-bottomed pot over high heat until hot but not smoking. Season the beef generously with salt and pepper. Add the beef to the pot and cook until browned on all sides, 6 to 8 minutes. (You may have to do this in batches.) Transfer the beef to a plate and set aside.

2. Add the onions to the pot, season with salt and pepper, and lower the heat to medium. Cook, stirring, for 10 minutes, until lightly browned. Add the celery, diced carrots, and garlic. Cook, stirring, for 5 to 6 minutes, until the onions begin to

caramelize. Add the fresh and dried mushrooms, thyme, and bay leaves, and cook, stirring, for 1 to 2 minutes.

3. Return the beef to the pot. Pour in the beer and broth, adding more broth or water, if necessary, to cover the meat. Bring to a boil over high heat, and then reduce the heat and simmer until the meat is fork-tender, 1½ to 2 hours.

4. Use tongs or a slotted spoon to transfer the beef to a plate and cover with aluminum foil to keep it warm. Bring the liquid to a boil over high heat. Let boil for 2 to 3 minutes, skimming any scum that rises to the surface. Add carrot pieces and boil until the liquid is thickened and the carrots are tender, about 12 minutes.

5. Use tongs or a slotted spoon to fish out and discard the thyme and bay leaves. Season the stew to taste with salt and pepper. Return the meat to the pot and warm it through over medium-low heat for 5 minutes. Alternatively, if not serving immediately, let cool, cover, and refrigerate for a few days or freeze for up to 1 month. Reheat before proceeding.

6. To serve, divide the stew among warm 8 bowls and top each serving with parsley.

Cuban-Style
Flank Steak and Pepper Stew

■ *Serves 6* ■

This is my version of a classic Cuban stew, made by combining slow-cooked flank steak with long-simmered peppers, onions, and tomato. The original dish is called *ropa vieja,* or "old clothes," because the shredded meat and sliced vegetables suggest tattered rags. Most *ropa vieja* recipes stew the steak with onions and peppers in simmering water, but canned chicken broth ups the flavor ante considerably. There are many ways to make this stew—some recipes use capers, some add red wine, and so on. Many leave out the tomato, but I love the way it tangs up the whole thing. Every cook seems to have his or her own *ropa vieja* secret. Here's mine: For a little spice and heat, I add ground cumin to the beef's cooking liquid and, at the last-minute, Tabasco sauce to the pepper and onion stew.

8 tablespoons olive oil

3 pounds flank steak, cut crosswise into 6 pieces

Coarse salt

Freshly ground black pepper

3 large Spanish onions, 1 peeled and cut into large dice, 2 peeled, halved, and sliced

3 bell peppers (green, red, or a combination) seeded, 1 cut into large dice, 2 sliced lengthwise

1 tablespoon distilled white vinegar (page 246)

About 1 quart store-bought reduced-sodium chicken broth, homemade Chicken Stock (page 244), or water

2 bay leaves

1 teaspoon black peppercorns

Pinch of ground cumin

3 cloves garlic, peeled and thinly sliced

2 tablespoons tomato paste

1½ cups canned crushed tomatoes with their liquid

½ teaspoon Tabasco sauce

1. Heat 2 tablespoons of the olive oil in a large pot over high heat until hot but not smoking. Season the flank steak with salt and pepper. Add half of the steak to the pan

and brown on all sides, about 5 minutes. Transfer the meat to a plate and set aside. Repeat using 2 more tablespoons oil and the remaining steak, transferring the browned meat to the plate.

2. Add 2 more tablespoons of the olive oil to the pot and heat over high heat. Add the diced onion and pepper, season with salt and pepper, and cook, stirring, until they just begin to brown, about 4 minutes. Add the vinegar and stir, scraping up any browned bits stuck on the bottom of the pot. Pour in the broth and let it come to a boil over high heat. Add the bay leaves, peppercorns, and cumin, and season with salt and pepper.

3. Return the steak to the pot. If the liquid does not come up to the top of the steak, add just enough broth or water so that it does (but do not drown the steak; you want the topmost piece just barely submerged).

4. When the liquid returns to a boil, cover the pot, lower the heat, and simmer until the meat is fork tender, about 2½ hours. Remove the pot from the heat and let the meat cool in the liquid for 30 minutes.

5. Transfer the meat to a plate. Strain the liquid and discard the solids. Let the liquid rest for 5 minutes, then spoon off and discard any fat that rises to the surface. Shred the meat by hand, pulling off and discarding any remaining fat. The meat and liquid can be cooled, covered, and refrigerated separately overnight. Let come to room temperature before proceeding.

6. Wipe out the pot, add the remaining 2 tablespoons olive oil, and heat over medium-low heat. Add the sliced onions and peppers and the garlic, and season with salt and pepper. Cook, stirring occasionally, until the onions and peppers are very soft, but not browned, about 20 minutes.

7. Add the tomato paste to the pot and stir for 2 minutes to coat the other ingredients. Add the tomatoes and 6 cups of the reserved beef cooking liquid and bring the liquid to a boil over high heat. Then lower the heat and let the liquid simmer until slightly thickened and richly flavored, about 15 minutes. Return the meat to the pot and stir it into the stew. Taste and adjust the seasoning with salt and pepper. If not serving immediately, let cool, cover, and refrigerate for a few days or freeze for up to 1 month. Reheat before proceeding.

8. To serve, divide the stew among 6 plates.

Beef Bourguignon

■ *Serves 6* ■

Many recipes in this chapter boil classic French preparations down to their essence, but it would be difficult to shorten the formula for one of the granddaddies of all beef stews, the hearty, vinous (more specifically, Burgundian) *boeuf bourguignon*. Beef bourguignon is a thinner stew than most we encounter today, largely because it's supposed to be made with a light-bodied red wine such as a Beaujolais or Pinot Noir. I've lightened it up even more with an addition of white vinegar, but otherwise it's fairly traditional. This is a great recipe to call on when you're hankering for a basic beef stew. Serve it atop egg noodles (page 217).

3 pounds beef chuck, cut into 2-inch
    chunks, trimmed of fat
Coarse salt
Freshly ground black pepper
½ pound slab bacon (page 241), cut
    into ¼-inch strips
3 cloves garlic, peeled and sliced
2 tablespoons plus 1½ teaspoons all-
    purpose flour
1½ cups red wine

1 tablespoon distilled white vinegar
    (page 246)
3 cups store-bought, reduced-sodium
    beef broth
1 pound white mushrooms, trimmed
    and quartered
1 large carrot, peeled and cut into
    small dice
1 pound pearl onions, peeled
1 teaspoon chopped fresh thyme leaves

1. Season the meat with salt and pepper. Set aside.

2. Cook the bacon in a large, heavy-bottomed pot over medium-high heat, stirring, until it is browned and has rendered enough fat to coat the bottom of the pot, about 7 minutes. Add the beef and garlic and cook, stirring, until the beef is browned on all sides, about 12 minutes.

3. Add the flour and stir to coat the meat, about 2 minutes. Add the red wine, white vinegar, and beef broth, stirring to prevent lumps. Bring to a simmer and add the mushrooms, carrot, onions, and thyme. Bring to a boil over high heat, and then lower the heat and simmer until the meat is very tender and the flavors are well integrated, 1 to 1½ hours. Taste and adjust seasoning with salt and pepper if necessary. If not serving immediately, let cool, cover, and refrigerate for a few days or freeze for up to 1 month. Reheat before proceeding.

4. To serve, ladle some stew into each of 6 warm bowls.

Beef Stroganoff

■ Serves 6 ■

The Russian beef Stroganoff is a dish in which thin strips of beef are cooked in a creamy, white-wine-based sauce with onions and mushrooms. It traditionally includes paprika, but to me it's all about the creamy mushroom sauce, which is intensified here with porcini mushroom powder replacing the paprika. (This fancy-sounding, delicious dust is easily made at home with dried porcini mushrooms—see the note at the end of the recipe.)

As a believer in not taking 30 minutes to accomplish what you can do in 10, I'm always looking for ways to quicken the cooking process. Here, I recommend working as you would if preparing a stir-fry, letting the pan get very hot. This way, the beef will cook quickly and the mushroom powder will be seared into it. To prevent scorching, keep the ingredients moving by stirring and shaking the pan.

2 pounds beef tenderloin, cut into thin, 1-inch strips
Coarse salt
Freshly ground black pepper
3 tablespoons porcini powder
2 tablespoons unsalted butter
2 tablespoons olive oil
½ medium onion, peeled and thinly sliced
2 cloves garlic, peeled and minced
20 white mushrooms, thinly sliced

2 tablespoons all-purpose flour
1 cup dry white wine
1½ cups store-bought, reduced-sodium beef broth
2 tablespoons green peppercorns packed in brine, rinsed and drained
½ cup sour cream
1 tablespoon chopped fresh chives
1 tablespoon chopped fresh tarragon leaves

1. Season the beef with salt, pepper, and the porcini powder and set aside.

2. Heat the butter and oil in a large, heavy-bottomed pot over high heat until the butter just begins to brown. Add the beef strips and brown quickly, moving the pot and shaking the beef around as you would if stir-frying. The beef should cook very

quickly, about 2 minutes; as soon as it's browned, transfer with tongs or a slotted spoon to a plate and set aside.

3. Add the onion and garlic to the pot and sauté until softened, about 2 minutes. Add the mushrooms and sauté until they begin to give off their liquid, about 4 minutes. Add the all-purpose flour and stir to coat the other ingredients, but do not let the flour brown.

4. Add the white wine gradually, stirring to prevent lumps. Add the beef broth gradually, still stirring. Bring to a boil, and let reduce and thicken for 2 minutes. Stir in the green peppercorns and sour cream. Lower the heat and return the beef to the pot. If not serving immediately, let cool, cover, and refrigerate for a few days or freeze for up to 1 month. Reheat before proceeding.

5. To serve, add the chives and tarragon and toss well. Divide among 6 warm plates and serve at once.

PORCINI POWDER

To make about 3 tablespoons of porcini powder, preheat the oven to 275°F. Spread the contents of a 1½-ounce package of dried porcini mushrooms on a baking sheet and bake in the oven until completely dried, 10 to 12 minutes. Remove from the oven, let cool, and grind in a coffee grinder or spice mill until you have a fine powder. Store in an empty spice jar, plastic container, or sealed plastic bag in a cool, dry place for up to 6 months. This is an excellent addition to soups and pasta sauces that feature mushrooms. A tablespoon will add plenty of flavor to most of the recipes in this book, but you may want a bit more if you love mushrooms.

Lamb Pasticcio

Serves 8

Pasticcio is an Italian casserole, sort of a free-form cousin of lasagna. My version is even more casual than the original, not bothering to layer the individual components. The result may remind you of a sophisticated version of that beefaroni they served in your junior-high cafeteria, which—if you're like me—you secretly remember more fondly that you'd ever admit. This is equally delicious with ground beef or ham.

2 large egg yolks
2 tablespoons olive oil
2 pounds ground lamb
Coarse salt
Freshly ground black pepper
½ large Spanish onion, peeled and cut
    into small dice
1 cup chopped, roasted tomato
    (page 231)
1 tablespoon tomato paste
2 tablespoons chopped fresh flat-leaf
    parsley leaves

2 tablespoons chopped fresh oregano
    leaves
8 tablespoons (1 stick) unsalted butter
¾ cup all-purpose flour
1 quart whole milk
1 cup freshly grated Parmesan cheese
1 pound ditalini or penette pasta,
    cooked until just al dente and
    drained (page 217)

1. Preheat the broiler. Put the egg yolks in a bowl and set aside. Season the lamb generously with salt and pepper.

2. Heat the olive oil in a large, heavy-bottomed pot over medium-high heat until hot but not smoking. Add the onion and cook until softened, about 4 minutes. Add the lamb and cook, breaking it up with a wooden spoon, until browned, about 10 minutes. Transfer the lamb-onion mixture to a bowl and stir in the roasted tomato, tomato paste, parsley, and oregano. Set aside.

3. Wipe out the pot, add the butter, and cook over medium heat until the butter is completely melted. Add the flour a little at a time, whisking it into the butter to incorporate thoroughly without making lumps. Slowly drizzle in the milk, letting it come briefly into contact with the bottom of the hot pot to warm it a bit before whisking it into the mixture. Add a few tablespoons of the hot mixture to the bowl with the egg yolk and whisk it in, then pour the entire mixture into the pot. Whisk in the Parmesan.

4. Place a casserole in the oven to warm it. Spoon about 1 cup of the béchamel sauce into a bowl and set aside. Stir the reserved lamb and the pasta into the remaining béchamel in the hot pot. Remove the casserole from the oven and transfer the contents of the pot into it. Top with the reserved béchamel, using a spatula or the back of a spoon to spread it evenly over the top of the casserole. If not serving immediately, let cool, cover, and refrigerate for a few days or freeze for up to 1 month. Reheat before proceeding.

5. Return the casserole to the oven and broil until lightly browned on top, about 2 minutes. Serve the pasticcio family style from the center of the table.

VARIATIONS

Pasticcio with Ground Sausage

For a fennel-tinged or spicier pasticcio, replace the ground lamb with an equal quantity of sweet or hot Italian sausage removed from its casing.

Andrew and Caitlin's Soppressata Lasagna

■ *Serves 8* ■

My co-author, Andrew Friedman, and his wife Caitlin devised this decadent lasagna rather spontaneously, during a trip through their local supermarket. As he tells the tale, they were planning on making lasagna for dinner one night, and got the idea to use slices of soppressata (a slightly-spicy, salami-like Italian cold cut made from cured pork shoulder) in place of ground beef as they strolled past the deli counter. What was to have been a basic lasagna Bolognese (featuring a red meat sauce) became something totally different as they finished shopping, deciding to add mushrooms and spinach in the produce department, and ricotta as they perused the dairy fridge. By the end of their tour, the dish they had in mind no longer included tomatoes at all. The use of a cold cut like soppressata in lasagna is highly unusual, but the flavor it produces tastes familiar because so many lasagnas feature ground meat. It also adds a pleasing saltiness to the entire dish.

1 tablespoon unsalted butter
1½ cups ricotta cheese
5 tablespoons olive oil
Coarse salt
Freshly ground black pepper
1 teaspoon crushed red pepper
3 cloves garlic, peeled and minced
12 ounces white mushrooms, cut into small dice

½ pound fresh spinach, stemmed, well washed, drained, and chopped
12 dried lasagna noodles (about ½ pound)
¼ pound thinly sliced soppressata
6 ounces fresh mozzarella cheese, grated (2 cups)
½ cup freshly grated Parmesan cheese

1. Preheat the oven to 350°F. Grease an 8-inch square baking dish with the butter.

2. Put the ricotta and 2 tablespoons of the olive oil in a medium bowl. Season with salt, black pepper, and the crushed red pepper. Stir and set aside.

3. Bring a large pot of salted water to a boil over high heat. Fill a medium bowl halfway with ice water and set aside.

4. While the water is coming to a boil, heat the remaining 3 tablespoons olive oil in a large sauté pan over medium-high heat. Add the garlic and cook for 1 minute. Add the mushrooms, season with salt and pepper, and sauté until they begin to give off their liquid, about 5 minutes. Stir in the spinach, and cook until wilted, about 1 minute. Remove the pan from the heat and set aside to cool.

5. Add the lasagna noodles to the boiling water and cook until just al dente, about 12 minutes. (You may need to do this in batches.) Drain the pasta and immediately dunk the noodles into the bowl of ice water to cool them and keep them from curling.

6. Drain the cooled mushroom and spinach mixture and add it to the seasoned ricotta.

7. Arrange a layer of pasta in the bottom of the buttered dish (you may need to trim the noodles to fit). Top with one-third of the soppressata, one-third of the ricotta mixture, and one-quarter of the mozzarella. Repeat twice, pressing down each layer gently. Then top with a final layer of pasta, topping it with mozzarella and the parmesan. If not serving immediately, let cool, cover with plastic wrap, and refrigerate for a few days or freeze for up to 1 month. Bring to room temperature before proceeding.

8. Cover the dish with aluminum foil and bake in the oven for 30 minutes. Remove the foil and cook for another 10 to 15 minutes, until the lasagna is golden brown and crispy on top.

9. Remove from the oven, let rest for 10 minutes, cut into individual portions, and serve family style from the center of the table.

VARIATION

Salami Lasagna
If you can't put your hands on soppressata, use a thinly sliced salami in its place.

Venison Chili

■ Serves 10 ■

I was delighted to discover the subtle quality farm-raised venison brings to chili, the meat's gently gamy flavor taking the place of the more pronounced flavor of ground beef.

If you've never made venison, this is a good way to introduce it in your kitchen because it's difficult to overcook it here. (There's a fine line between perfectly cooked and overcooked venison, which makes grilling venison chops or steaks a daunting task for some home cooks.) If you are unable to find venison, this recipe is also delicious made with coarsely ground, lean beef. This makes a deliberately large batch of chili; people seem unable to resist seconds, and it's a favorite for leftovers.

Serve this over brown rice (page 211).

2 pounds boneless venison leg meat,
    coarsely ground
Coarse salt
Freshly ground black pepper
7 cloves garlic, peeled and minced
2 tablespoons olive oil
1 large carrot, cut into small dice
1 medium Spanish onion, cut into
    small dice
2 stalks celery, cut into small dice
1 tablespoon chopped fresh thyme
    leaves
¼ cup distilled white vinegar
    (page 246)
¼ cup tomato paste
1 cup dark beer

One 14½-ounce can stewed tomatoes
4 plum tomatoes, chopped
Half a 7-ounce can chipotle chiles in
    adobo (about 5 peppers), finely
    chopped
1 cup store-bought, reduced-sodium
    beef broth
1 teaspoon ground cumin
1 teaspoon ground coriander
¼ teaspoon cayenne pepper
1 teaspoon sugar
1 bay leaf
Two 15-ounce cans red kidney beans,
    drained and rinsed
½ cup sour cream, optional
3 scallions, thinly sliced, optional

1. Put the venison in a bowl and season with 5 teaspoons salt, 2 teaspoons black pepper, and half of the garlic. Set aside for 30 minutes.

2. Heat the olive oil in a large, heavy-bottomed pot over medium-high heat. Add the venison and cook, stirring, until browned, 3 to 5 minutes.

3. Add the carrot, onion, and celery, season with salt and pepper, and cook, stirring, until the vegetables are softened, about 5 minutes. Stir in the remaining garlic and the thyme and cook for 5 minutes. Add the vinegar to the pot and bring to a boil, scraping the bottom of the pot to loosen any browned bits. Add the tomato paste and 1 tablespoon salt and cook for 2 minutes, stirring to coat the other ingredients with the paste and integrate all the flavors.

4. Add the beer, raise the heat until the mixture boils, then lower the heat and simmer until the beer is reduced by half, about 4 minutes. Add the tomatoes, chipotle peppers, broth, cumin, coriander, cayenne pepper, sugar, bay leaf, and 1 tablespoon salt to the pot, stir, and let simmer gently for 45 minutes.

5. Add the kidney beans to the pot and cook for another 15 minutes, or until the chili is thickened.

6. Pick out and discard the thyme sprigs and bay leaf. If not serving immediately, let cool, cover, and refrigerate for a few days or freeze for up to 1 month. Reheat before proceeding.

7. To serve, divide the chili among 10 bowls and garnish with the sour cream and scallion, if desired.

Rabbit Stew with Marjoram and Vermouth

■ Serves 6 ■

Cooking or eating rabbit may be a leap of faith for some of you, but it's a leap I encourage you to take. I always have rabbit on my restaurant menu for those who appreciate its lean meat, which is especially well suited to stewing. Here, rabbit is paired with marjoram and vermouth, best known as the key component of a martini, whose botanical components (it's made from flowers and seeds) are the perfect match for the delicate flavor and texture of rabbit.

10 plum tomatoes, diced
Coarse salt
Freshly ground black pepper
Sugar
2 tablespoons unsalted butter
2 tablespoons olive oil
2 rabbits (about 2 pounds each),
    cut by your butcher into 5 pieces
    each (front legs, back legs, and
    saddle)
12 cloves garlic, peeled and sliced
2 large Spanish onions, peeled,
    quartered, and thinly sliced

2 cups dry white wine
2 cups dry vermouth
2 tablespoons distilled white vinegar
    (page 246)
About 2 quarts store-bought,
    reduced-sodium chicken broth
    or homemade Chicken Stock
    (page 244)
4 teaspoons chopped fresh marjoram
    leaves
1⅓ cups pastina (page 217)

1. Thirty minutes before you want to cook, put the tomatoes in a bowl and season with salt, pepper, and a pinch of sugar. Set aside.

2. Preheat oven to 325°F.

3. Heat the butter and oil in a large, heavy-bottomed pot over medium-high heat. Season the rabbit with salt and pepper. Add the rabbit pieces and cook until browned on all sides, about 10 minutes. Transfer them to a plate and set aside.

4. Drain all but 2 tablespoons of the fat from the pan. Add the garlic and onions and cook for 30 seconds. Add the wine, vermouth, and vinegar, bring to a boil, and cook until the liquid is reduced by half. Add the reserved tomatoes, stir, and cook for 3 to 4 minutes. Taste and adjust the seasoning of the liquid with salt and pepper, if necessary.

5. Return the rabbit pieces to the pot in a single layer on top of the vegetables. Add the broth; if it doesn't completely cover the rabbit pieces, add more broth or water. Sprinkle the marjoram on top. Bring the liquid to a boil over high heat. Transfer the pot to the oven and braise for 18 to 20 minutes until the meat is firm to the touch. Transfer the saddles to a plate and let the legs cook another 5 minutes, and then transfer them to the plate. If not serving immediately, let cool, cover, and refrigerate the rabbit and sauce separately for up to a few days. Reheat the sauce and bring the rabbit to room temperature before proceeding.

6. Add the pastina and cook for 6 to 7 minutes until the pastina is al dente. Return the rabbit pieces to the pot to reheat for 2 to 3 minutes.

7. To serve, divide the rabbit and stew among 6 warm bowls.

VARIATION

Chicken Stew with Marjoram and Vermouth

You can substitute 2 quartered chickens for the rabbit, but increase the browning time at the beginning of the recipe to about 15 minutes to account for the chicken's skin.

Tripe with Tomatoes, Thyme, and Oregano

■ *Serves 6* ■

Most people don't eat tripe, which leaves more for those of us who love it. I learned to appreciate its richly gelatinous texture as a child, and developed an even deeper fondness for it when I worked in France. One of my favorite ways to enjoy it is in a tomato sauce that uses some of the tripe's powerfully flavored cooking liquid, oregano, thyme, and a dash of white vinegar. This is a two-day process but worth every moment of patient anticipation.

Tripe

4 pounds tripe (if frozen, allow to thaw thoroughly)	2 tablespoons black peppercorns
	3 sprigs thyme
1 carrot, peeled and coarsely chopped	1 bay leaf
1 Spanish onion, peeled and quartered	⅔ cup distilled white vinegar (page 246)
3 cloves garlic, smashed and peeled	2 tablespoons coarse salt

1. Put the tripe in a large, heavy-bottomed pot with the carrot, onion, garlic, peppercorns, thyme, and bay leaf. Add enough cold water to cover by 3 or 4 inches. Add the vinegar and salt and bring the liquid to a boil over high heat. Skim any scum that rises to the surface, then lower the heat and simmer for 3 to 4 hours. To test for doneness, remove a piece of tripe from the pot using tongs. Get your fingers good and cold in a bowl of ice water. Pinch the tripe. If your fingers can easily push through the meat and meet in the middle, it's done.

2. Strain the tripe in a fine-mesh strainer set over a bowl. Reserve 1 quart of the strained cooking liquid, set aside to cool, and discard the rest of the liquid. Remove the tripe from the strainer and discard the other solids. Cool the tripe under cold running water. Wrap the tripe in plastic wrap and pour the cooking liquid into an airtight container; refrigerate for up to 24 hours.

Tomato Sauce

4 plum tomatoes, diced

Coarse salt

Freshly ground black pepper

Sugar

2 tablespoons olive oil

½ Spanish onion, peeled and cut into small dice

1 large carrot, peeled and cut into small dice

2 stalks celery, peeled and cut into small dice

3 cloves garlic, peeled and thinly sliced

1 tablespoon tomato paste

½ cup dry white wine

2 tablespoons distilled white vinegar (page 246)

1 teaspoon chopped fresh thyme leaves

½ teaspoon chopped fresh oregano leaves

1 quart store-bought, reduced-sodium chicken broth or homemade Chicken Stock (page 244)

2 tablespoons chopped fresh flat-leaf parsley leaves

Grated parmesan cheese

1. Thirty minutes before you want to cook, put the tomatoes in a bowl and season with salt, pepper, and a pinch of sugar. Set aside.

2. Heat the oil in a large, heavy-bottomed pot over medium-high heat. Add the onion, carrot, celery, and garlic and sauté, stirring, until softened but not browned, 10 to 12 minutes. Add the tomato paste and stir to coat the other ingredients. Cook for 2 minutes. Add the wine and vinegar, bring to a boil, and cook until nearly all of the liquid has evaporated.

3. Add the reserved tomatoes, thyme, and oregano and stir to incorporate. Stir in the chicken broth and reserved tripe cooking liquid, bring to boil, and then lower the heat and simmer until the flavors are nicely concentrated, 20 to 25 minutes.

4. Meanwhile, cut the tripe into bite-size triangles or strips. Add them to the liquid and cook until warmed through and tender, about 10 minutes. Season with salt and pepper if necessary. If not serving immediately, let cool, cover, and refrigerate for a few days or freeze for up to 1 month. Reheat before proceeding.

5. Divide the tripe among 6 warm bowls, top each serving with a generous amount of sauce, and pass the Parmesan alongside.

VARIATION

Tripe with White Beans and Tubetti

Cook 1 cup dried tubetti until al dente (see page 217). Drain and add it and one 15-ounce can drained cannellini beans to the pot during the last 10 minutes of cooking.

Large Cuts
and **Catches**

Many of the recipes in the previous chapters are versatile; suitable for a first-course, a main-course, or even a side-dish. But the ones that follow are non-negotiable: They're the stars of the show, the main event. They're also some of my favorites, the ones that hark back to those dishes I grew up on and that satisfy me when I'm feeling the most unabashedly hungry and carnivorous.

In these pages you'll find such familiar dishes as Slow-Cooked Chicken in a Pot (page 158); Baked Chicken with Bacon, Mushrooms, and Pearl Onions (page 150); and Moroccan-Spice-Braised Lamb Shank (page 167). These are the kinds of dishes you can tell will be delicious just by looking at them.

Many of these dishes follow a similar cooking progression: Where meats and poultry are concerned, browning or searing is often a crucial first step—a sort of culinary cauterization that leaves behind tasty caramelized bits that contribute essential flavor to the sauce. Which leads us to the second similarity: As a lot of these dishes cook, the juices from the meats combine with the flavors of the other ingredients (wine, vegetables, broth) to yield a rich sauce perfectly suited to the meat.

You'll also notice that many of the recipes feature a similar group of ingredients. If I ever find myself accepting a Lifetime Achievement Award, I'll be thanking red wine, distilled white vinegar, and canned Italian tomatoes. And I'll save my biggest nod for bacon and other pork products, which I use compulsively to add salty, smoky flavor to all sorts of dishes. (There are notes on these and other ingredients I love on pages 239 to 246.) In fact, if I can't make it to the ceremony, I might just send a pig to accept the award in my place.

Because these ingredients are used over and over, the liquids they produce might seem like an almost incidental by-product, but they're not. You'll notice significant differences in the amount of distilled white vinegar called for in, say, the Classic Braised Beef Brisket (page 172) and the Braised Pork Shank (page 184). Each and every braising liquid and sauce in this chapter has been carefully tested. You might be just as surprised by the variety of flavors these ingredients can produce as you are by how many dishes you can cook up in one pot. For a good comparison, think about how many Italian recipes call for olive oil, tomatoes, garlic, and Parmesan cheese; it might be easier to name the ones that don't.

I also love many less-familiar foods, and one of my goals in this chapter is to introduce you to meats and cuts you might not know—or know how to cook—such as squab, oxtail, beef cheeks, pork shank, and veal breast. I firmly believe that they are all worth discovering and, because they're all cooked in one pot, the following recipes make it easy for you to succeed magnificently with them. Aside from browning, and some careful monitoring for doneness, all of the work involved, all of the tasting and judgement, has to do with the sauce or braising liquid rather than the actual meat.

In other words, my philosophy is this: If you can follow the technique provided by these recipes, you can cook almost any large cut of meat.

Another great convenience of these recipes is that almost all can be prepared at least a day in advance. Even for the fish dishes, cooking liquids can be prepared and refrigerated overnight.

When making the dishes in this chapter, the proper equipment is critical. Almost all of the poultry and meats call for an initial browning, and a heavy-bottomed pot enables you to do this without leaving half of the meat seared onto the pot itself.

Finally, I encourage you to use the most important and inexpensive kitchen tool of all, your own taste buds. Because virtually all these dishes are made in cooking liquid, you have the opportunity to correct, improve, and perfect the dish at every stage of the process. So taste often and season mercilessly until what reaches your tongue puts a smile on your face.

Simmered Shrimp Sauté with Shiitake Mushrooms and Scallions

■ *Serves 4* ■

My favorite way to eat shrimp is the classic shrimp cocktail where they are cooked in a great deal of water and emerge terrifically tender. Conversely, I could list about a million things I don't like about so-called shrimp scampi (not least of which is its name, which translates to the redundant "shrimp shrimp"). Semantics aside, I object to such quick-sautéed shrimp dishes because the high heat and stingy amount of liquid often causes the meat to seize up and toughen. The same will happen with most shellfish, including lobster; the one major exception is sea scallops, which respond well to a searing over high heat.

So, the idea behind this recipe is to combine the tender, succulent result of shrimp cooked in a generous amount of liquid with the appeal of cooking them in something more flavorful than water, in this case a buttery broth enhanced by white wine, garlic, scallion, and basil. This Asian-accented dish pairs well with linguine (page 219) or Israeli couscous (page 209).

2 tablespoons unsalted butter, at room temperature, plus 4 tablespoons unsalted butter, chilled and cut into small dice

2 cloves garlic, peeled and thinly sliced

4 large shiitake mushroom caps, very thinly sliced

Coarse salt

Freshly ground black pepper

2 plum tomatoes, cut into small dice

3 scallions, white and light green parts, thinly sliced on a bias

½ cup dry white wine

1 cup store-bought, reduced-sodium chicken broth or homemade Chicken Stock (page 244)

1 teaspoon freshly squeezed lemon juice

2 pounds peeled, butterflied, deveined large shrimp (see note, page 87)

1 tablespoon capers, rinsed and drained

2 tablespoons chopped fresh flat-leaf parsley leaves

2 tablespoons chopped fresh basil leaves

1. Melt the 2 tablespoons room-temperature butter in a wide, deep sauté pan over medium heat. Add the garlic and cook gently until softened but not browned, 2 to 3 minutes. Add the mushrooms, season with salt and pepper, and cook for 1 minute. Add the tomatoes and scallions and cook gently until softened, 3 to 4 minutes.

2. Turn the heat up to high. Just as the butter starts to sizzle, add the wine. Boil until the liquid has evaporated, 1 to 2 minutes. Add the chicken broth and lemon juice and bring to a boil, and then lower the heat and simmer for 2 minutes. Add the diced, cold butter, a few pieces at a time, swirling it in as it's added. (Do not allow the liquid to boil once the butter has been added. The sauce should look like a buttery broth; if it appears excessively thick, stir in a few tablespoons of hot water.) Taste and adjust the seasoning if necessary.

3. Season the shrimp with salt and pepper, and add them to the pan, making sure to immerse them in the liquid. Cook over medium-low heat just below a simmer for 3 to 4 minutes, or until the shrimp are pink and firm. Add the capers, toss, and cook for 30 seconds. Add the parsley and basil and toss to combine. Remove from the heat.

4. To serve, divide the shrimp and sauce among 4 warm bowls.

VARIATIONS

Simmered Shrimp Sauté with Chanterelle Mushrooms and Leeks

For a more French-leaning recipe, replace the sliced shiitake mushrooms with small chanterelles or halved large ones and replace the scallions with the white portion of one large leek, quartered lengthwise, cut into ½-inch pieces, rinsed, and dried.

Simmered Shrimp Sauté with Cilantro or Tarragon

Replace the basil with cilantro or tarragon for a quick but marked change in flavor.

Olive-Oil-Poached Red Snapper with Tomato and Scallions

■ *Serves 4* ■

If you think that poaching fish can only produce a bland result that smacks of health spas and sensory deprivation, then you haven't poached in olive oil. The oil creates a gentle bath that, because of the oil's viscosity, keeps the fish's moisture intact. The result is a distinctly silky luxury. The phrase "melts in your mouth" gets overused, but this snapper pretty much does just that. (The technique is a variation on confit, the method used to preserve meats and poultry by slow-cooking them in their own fat. Only here we're using oil for its rich flavor and we're not preserving.)

If it seems like you're cooking in a large quantity of oil, keep in mind that while the fish takes on the flavor of the oil, it doesn't become saturated as it would if you were frying. And olive oil is good for you; it's a monounsaturated fat full of antioxidants. You will need a kitchen thermometer to keep the oil temperature constant while making this dish.

This dish should be cooked just before it's served because it cannot be reheated. It can, however, be kept aside for an hour or two and served at room temperature.

Snapper is a full-flavored fish to begin with, and this is an exceptionally rich treatment, so the portions are intentionally small. Serve this with something light, such as boiled potatoes or some simply dressed greens.

4 plum tomatoes, peeled, seeded
   (page 245), and cut into ¼-inch dice
Coarse salt
Freshly ground black pepper
Four 6-ounce red snapper fillets,
   ideally 1 inch thick, skin on
Garlic powder
½ cup chopped fresh dill
About 1 quart olive oil, for poaching

3 cloves garlic, peeled and minced
4 scallions, white parts plus 1 inch of
   green, thinly cut on the bias
1 tablespoon dry white wine
1 teaspoon chopped fresh tarragon
   leaves
1 lemon, halved
Fleur de sel (see note, page 145)
½ cup fresh flat-leaf parsley leaves

1. About 30 minutes before you want to cook, put the tomatoes in a bowl and season with salt and pepper. Give a good toss and set aside at room temperature. Take the snapper out of the refrigerator so that it warms to room temperature. Season the fillets all over with salt, pepper, garlic powder, and dill.

2. Pour 1½ inches of olive oil into a heavy-bottomed pot just big enough to hold the fillets comfortably in a single layer. Warm the oil very gently over low heat until it reaches a temperature of 100°F. (It's normal to overshoot the desired temperature. Don't worry about it: Just turn off the flame and place the pot on an idle burner until it cools to the right temperature.)

3. Double check that the fillets are at room temperature. (If you immerse cold fish into the oil, the oil will cool too quickly.) Gently immerse the fish into the oil. Let sit, off the heat, for about 25 minutes, depending on the thickness of the fish. The fish is done when it flakes easily and is opaque throughout. If not done, set the pot over very low heat for a few minutes.

4. After the fish has been poaching for about 20 minutes, prepare the sauce: Transfer 1 tablespoon of the poaching oil to a sauté pan and warm it over medium heat. Add the reserved tomatoes, garlic, scallions, and white wine to the pan. Simmer, stirring often, for about 5 minutes. Stir in the tarragon just before serving.

5. To serve, place 1 fillet on each of 4 warm dinner plates. Top with some of the sauce, a squeeze of lemon, a pinch of *fleur de sel,* and some parsley leaves.

VARIATIONS

This preparation will also give you stellar results with bass, salmon, or turbot.

TOMORROW'S TABLE

Flake any leftover fish and toss it with lemon juice for the basis of a rich Niçoise-style salad like those served in the South of France. Complete the salad with greens, boiled green beans, boiled potatoes, hard-cooked eggs, and sliced, marinated artichoke hearts.

Simmered Shrimp Sauté with Shiitake Mushrooms and Scallions

Macaroni and Goat Cheese
(page 90)

Lentil and Garlic Sausage Stew
(page 110)

Shrimp Stew with Leeks
(page 102)

Extra-Smoky New England Clam Chowder
(page 48)

Ham Hock and Split Pea Soup
(page 66)

Andrew and Caitlin's Soppressata Lasagna
(page 126)

Moroccan-Spice-Braised Lamb Shank
(page 167)

Root Vegetable Stew with Cumin, Coriander, and Millet
(page 78)

Beef on a String Soup and Sandwich
(page 176)

Lamb Pasticcio
(page 124)

Baked Chicken with Bacon,
Mushrooms, and Pearl Onions
(page 150)

Portuguese-Style Pork Roast with Steamed Clams
(page 186)

Florentine Pot Roast with Red Wine,
Mushrooms, and Tomatoes
(page 178)

Baked Sea Bass, Papillote Style, with Lemon and Olives
(page 146)

CELERY SALAD

The poaching oil can also be used to make a tasty celery salad. Peel the outer ribs of a few celery stalks and cut the stalks ribbon-thin on the bias. Peel and thinly slice 1 medium red onion. Put the celery and onion in a bowl, add 1 teaspoon drained capers and a ½ bunch frisée lettuce. Add a few spoonfuls of the poaching liquid, season with salt and pepper, and hit it with a squeeze of lemon. Toss well and serve. You can make this salad truly luxurious by topping with it with crème fraîche and caviar.

FLEUR DE SEL

Fleur de sel, slightly coarse French sea salt, is often used as a final flourish on fish and meats because it offers a nice textural crunch and gentle salinity. It's not as salty as iodized or granulated salt and not as crystalline as coarse Kosher salt. It can really help bring out the individual flavors in a dish at the last second, even at the table, without distracting from them.

Baked Sea Bass, Papillote Style, with Lemon and Olives

■ *Serves 4* ■

This is a ridiculously easy preparation based on dishes cooked *en papillote,* a French technique that bakes a dish's ingredients—usually fish and vegetables—in a parchment-paper packet brushed with melted butter. In the right hands, this is a beautiful thing: The little packages puff up in a charming, almost regal way and turn golden-brown in the heat of the oven. And the presentation is dramatic: The paper is broken open right under the diner's nose, releasing a plume of aromatic steam. This technique has left quite a legacy: Dishes cooked *en papillote* were probably the first prepared, single-serving meal ever invented, an unlikely ancestor of Stouffer's frozen meals and Jiffy Pop popcorn. On a more personal note: I've always thought this technique was cool because it cooks a big paper package in the oven without causing a fire.

This recipe adapts the papillote concept, transferring it to a baking sheet and substituting a common modern convenience, aluminum foil, for the parchment paper. It also does away with the single-serving notion, cooking all of the fish together.

I recommend serving this with steamed couscous (page 208) or millet (page 209).

4 sea bass, snapper, or striped bass fillets (7 ounces each), skin on	2 cups assorted olives such as Niçoise, Kalamata, and Picholine, pitted
2 cloves garlic, peeled and very thinly sliced	2 tablespoons chopped fresh chives
2 tablespoons chopped fresh tarragon leaves	¼ cup extra-virgin olive oil
1 lemon, peeled and separated into segments (see note, page 147)	¼ cup dry white wine
	¼ cup bottled clam juice
	Coarse salt
	Freshly ground black pepper

1. Preheat the oven to 325°F. To keep the fish from curling when cooked, score the skin diagonally at 1-inch intervals using a razor blade or very sharp, very thin-bladed knife.

2. Line a rimmed baking sheet with aluminum foil. Scatter the garlic, tarragon, lemon segments, olives, and chives over the foil. Drizzle with the olive oil, wine, and clam juice. Season the fish fillets on both sides with salt and pepper and arrange, skin side up, in the pan without crowding. Cover with another sheet of aluminum foil and crimp the sheets of foil around the edges to seal the contents, pressing gently on the top to release any excess air.

3. Place the baking sheet in the oven and bake until the fish is very firm to the touch and opaque at the center, about 20 minutes. (To check, open the foil carefully at one edge and break a fillet open gently with a spatula. If the fish isn't done when you check it, reseal the foil and return the pan to the oven for another few minutes.)

4. To serve, remove the pan from the oven and carefully transfer 1 fish fillet to the center of each of 4 warm plates. Spoon some of the pan juices, olives, and lemon segments over and around the fish.

VARIATIONS

Baked Sea Bass with Tomato and Green Peppercorns

For a more colorful take on this idea with a pronounced saltiness, scatter ½ cup diced tomato in the pan along with the garlic, tarragon, lemon segments, olives, and chives, and add a tablespoon of green peppercorns packed in brine along with the olive oil, wine, and clam juice.

CITRUS SEGMENTS

To make peeled lemon, lime, or orange segments (called *suprêmes* in French), cut the top and bottom off the fruit. Stand it on 1 end and using a sharp knife, cut down along the sides, following the curve of the fruit and removing the peel, pith, and a little bit of the fruit so that the flesh is exposed. Cut between the membranes to separate the fruit into totally exposed segments. Carefully remove and discard the seeds.

Cod with Tomato, Saffron Broth, Leeks, and Couscous

■ *Serves 4* ■

A flaky, white fish enlivened with the bright flavors of tomato and saffron is, to my way of thinking, pure Mediterranean bliss. I recommend taking the sunny spirit of this dish a step further by serving it with baguette croutons spread with Aïoli (page 230). If you don't have baguette in the house, feel free to spread the aïoli on Melba toast. You heard me right, Melba toast. Go ahead; don't be a snob.

This recipe is delicious made with almost any thick cut of white-fleshed fish such as halibut or flounder. Stay away from more meaty fish like tuna and swordfish.

If you like to cook in advance, you can make the cooking liquid ahead of time, then reheat it when you're ready to poach the fish. But don't season the cod until just before cooking or the salt will rob it of some of its moisture.

3 large plum tomatoes, seeded (page 245) and cut into 1-inch dice

Coarse salt

Freshly ground black pepper

Pinch of sugar

4 boneless, skinless cod fillets (about 6 ounces each), ideally 1 inch thick

Garlic powder

¼ cup extra-virgin olive oil, plus more for serving

1 large Spanish onion, peeled, halved, and thinly sliced

3 medium leeks, tough green portion removed, thickest outer white layer removed, cut on a bias into 1-inch sections and washed well

4 cloves garlic, peeled and thinly sliced

1½ cups light, dry white wine, such as Pinot Blanc or Chablis

1 tablespoon distilled white vinegar (page 246)

One 16-ounce bottle clam juice

1 cup water

Pinch of saffron threads (page 55)

1½ cups couscous (page 208)

¼ cup chopped fresh flat-leaf parsley leaves

1. About 30 minutes before you plan to cook, put the tomatoes in a bowl and season with salt, pepper, and the sugar. Give a good toss and set aside at room temperature.

2. Generously season the cod on both sides with salt, pepper, and garlic powder. Set aside at room temperature.

3. Heat 2 tablespoons of the olive oil in a large, heavy-bottomed pot over medium heat until hot but not smoking. Add the onion, leeks, and garlic and cook until softened but not browned, 7 to 8 minutes. Add the reserved tomatoes and cook for 2 to 3 minutes, stirring well to incorporate the ingredients. Add the white wine and vinegar and stir, scraping up any browned bits that are stuck to the bottom of the pot. Raise the heat to high and cook for 2 minutes. Add the clam juice, water, and saffron and bring to a boil. Taste and season with more salt and pepper if necessary.

4. Put the couscous in a heatproof bowl. Taking care to not scoop up any solids, or as few solids as possible, ladle about 1 cup of hot liquid from the pot and pour over the couscous until it is covered it by 1 inch. Cover the bowl tightly with plastic wrap and set aside.

5. Lower the heat under the pot and carefully immerse the reserved cod pieces, one by one, into the simmering liquid. Cover and simmer gently for about 10 minutes, until you feel that with the pressure of a fork or a spoon the cod will come apart easily. If the center still offers resistance you need to cook it for a few more minutes.

6. A few minutes before the fish is done, fluff the couscous with a fork.

7. To serve, divide the couscous among 4 warm, wide, deep bowls. Carefully place 1 piece of cod over the couscous in each bowl. Ladle some broth over each portion, scatter some parsley over the top, and drizzle with extra-virgin olive oil.

VARIATIONS

This recipe offers an appealingly easy way to cook relatively inexpensive fish, such as scrod or halibut, and infuse it with flavor. It's also delicious with the more assertive flavor of bluefish or mackerel.

Baked Chicken with Bacon, Mushrooms, and Pearl Onions

■ *Serves 4* ■

There's a catch-all category of classic French recipes called *grand-mère* (grandmother), or *bonne femme,* which are hearty, rustic dishes, usually served right from the crock or casserole in which they were cooked. In other words, exactly the kind of homey food a French grandmother, or my grandmother for that matter, might prepare, and serve, simply, from the center of the table. These days, advertisers make a big deal of cookware that can go "from the oven to the table," but generations ago it was the standard—a wonderful bit of style that people took for granted.

Beyond this (optional) presentation, I think this recipe proves the point I was trying to make in the Introduction—that cooking once looked on as common has today become fashionable. (Of course, truly wise people like you and I have always found it delicious.) There's nothing unusual here, no secret ingredients or earth-shattering techniques, but you'll be hard-pressed to find someone who doesn't love this dish.

Serve this with Mashed Potatoes (page 221) or Polenta (page 210).

One 3-pound chicken, cut into 8 pieces
Coarse salt
Freshly ground black pepper
2 teaspoons olive oil
½ pound slab bacon (page 241), cut
    into ½-inch dice
12 cloves garlic, unpeeled
16 pearl onions, peeled

24 white mushrooms, trimmed
1 cup dry white wine
15 sprigs assorted herbs (such as
    parsley, thyme, rosemary,
    marjoram, and sage)
1 to 2 tablespoons all-purpose flour or
    cornstarch, optional

1. Preheat the oven to 325°F. Wash the chicken pieces under cold running water and pat dry with paper towels. Season the chicken all over with salt and pepper. Set aside.

2. Heat the olive oil and bacon over medium-high heat in a large, heavy-bottomed pot large enough to hold all of the ingredients. Cook until the bacon has browned and rendered enough fat to coat the bottom of the pot, about 5 minutes. Use a slotted spoon to transfer the bacon to a paper-towel-lined plate to drain, leaving as much fat as possible in the pot.

3. Add the chicken pieces, skin side down, and brown all over in the bacon fat, 4 to 5 minutes per side. (You may need to do this in batches.) Return the bacon to the pan, along with the garlic, onions, mushrooms, wine, and herb sprigs. Cover the pot and transfer it to the oven. Bake for 20 minutes, then remove the cover and bake for another 20 minutes.

4. Use tongs or a slotted spoon to transfer the chicken and vegetables from the pot to a warm platter. As you do, discard the herb sprigs. Skim any grease from the surface of the sauce, and then whisk in the flour or cornstarch to thicken it, if desired.

5. Return the chicken to the pot and serve family style from the center of the table, or divide the chicken pieces among 4 plates, spoon a good assortment of vegetables over each portion, and top with some sauce.

VARIATIONS

Baked Chicken with Red Wine, Tomatoes, Mushrooms, and Pearl Onions
Make this with red wine instead of white wine and add 5 chopped, seasoned plum tomatoes before adding the chicken to the pot in Step 3.

Game Bird with Bacon, Mushrooms, and Pearl Onions
You can substitute pheasant or guinea hen for the chicken, but bear in mind that they're leaner and therefore cook in a slightly shorter amount of time.

For a more pronounced mushroom flavor, add ½ cup dried porcini mushrooms (do not reconstitute them first) along with the bacon in Step 3.

Chicken in Hunter-Style Sauce

Serves 4

Most Americans seem to have heard of the Italian phrase *alla cacciatora,* but virtually nobody is able to define it. Strictly speaking, *alla cacciatora* means "hunter-style," but that doesn't really clear things up because all this means is that it uses a meat that's hunted (as in almost anything that walks or flies). The sauce is made by adding any number of vegetables to a base of tomatoes and onions, though some definitions insist that mushrooms are also a mandatory ingredient. Suffice it to say that *alla cacciatora* is one of those definitions that change from door to door throughout the country of my ancestors.

I've always associated chicken *alla cacciatora* not with Italy per se, but with Italian-Americans. So my version is very much defined by the favorite herb of that proud hyphenate—oregano. And I've taken my own liberties, adding what I'm sure is an unconventional alcohol in this context, vermouth, usually reserved for cooking rabbit, another of the hunter's favorite catches.

I recommend serving this with orzo (page 217).

2 to 3 very ripe, firm meaty tomatoes, or canned imported Italian plum tomatoes, cut up, with their juice (about 1½ cups)	¼ cup olive oil
	1 medium Spanish onion, peeled and cut into 8 wedges
Coarse salt	3 cloves garlic, peeled and thinly sliced
Freshly ground black pepper	1 cup dry white wine
One 3- to 4-pound chicken, cut into 8 pieces	1 cup dry vermouth
	¼ cup fresh oregano leaves

1. About 30 minutes before you want to cook, put the tomatoes in a bowl and season with salt and pepper. Give a good toss and set aside at room temperature.

2. Preheat the oven to 375°F.

3. Wash the chicken in cold running water and pat thoroughly dry with paper towels. Season generously with salt and pepper. Heat the oil in a wide, heavy-bottomed ovenproof pot over medium-high heat until hot but not smoking. Add the chicken pieces and brown well, 4 to 5 minutes per side. Use tongs or a slotted spoon to transfer the chicken pieces to a plate; set aside.

4. Add the onion and garlic to the pot and cook, stirring, until softened, about 6 minutes. Add the reserved tomatoes, toss well, and cook for 1 minute. Add the wine, vermouth, and oregano and cook for 1 minute more.

5. Return the chicken pieces to the pot, skin side up. Transfer to the oven and cook until a sharp, thin-bladed knife inserted near the bone reveals no red within and only the faintest trace of pink, if any, about 25 minutes for the breast pieces, 40 minutes for the others. As the pieces are done, transfer them to a plate, covering them with aluminum foil to keep them warm.

6. To serve, divide the chicken among 4 warm plates, spooning a good variety of vegetables over each portion.

VARIATION

Hunter-Style Rabbit

For a more rustic recipe, replace the chicken with rabbit and use chopped sage or marjoram in place of oregano.

TOMORROW'S TABLE

Fettuccine alla Cacciatora

If there's any leftover chicken, cut it up, return it to the sauce, heat gently, and toss with cooked fettuccine (page 219). Top with freshly grated Parmesan cheese.

Chicken Braised with Mushrooms

▪ Serves 8 ▪

This isn't a terribly complicated recipe, and—to be perfectly honest—there's nothing earth-shatteringly innovative about it. All I can tell you is that it tastes great. Chicken and mushrooms both have an amazing capacity to soak up the flavor of white wine, tingeing them with a pleasing acidity. The ingredient list below doesn't look like much but, trust me, it adds up to much more than the sum of its parts.

2 chickens (about 3 pounds each), quartered
Coarse salt
Freshly ground black pepper
½ cup olive oil
1 bottle (750 ml) dry white wine
1 tablespoon fresh thyme leaves
1½ quarts store-bought, reduced-sodium chicken broth or homemade Chicken Stock (page 244)

¼ cup dried porcini mushrooms (page 243), rinsed
4 cloves garlic, peeled and sliced, plus 8 cloves, unpeeled
1½ pounds small white mushrooms
2 tablespoons unsalted butter, optional

1. Preheat the oven to 400°F.

2. Wash the chicken pieces in cold running water and pat thoroughly dry with paper towels. Season generously with salt and pepper. Heat the olive oil in a large, heavy-bottomed ovenproof pot over medium-high heat until hot but not smoking. Add the chicken pieces and brown them all over, 4 to 5 minutes per side. (You may need to do this in batches.) Use tongs or a slotted spoon to transfer the chicken to a plate; set aside.

3. Remove the pot from the heat. Pour out and discard the fat. Return the pot to the stovetop, add the wine, and bring to a boil over medium-high heat, scraping up any browned bits stuck to the bottom of the pot. Add the thyme and cook for 1 to

2 minutes. Add the chicken broth, porcini, and garlic cloves. Stir in 1 tablespoon salt and 1 teaspoon pepper.

4. Return the chicken to the pot and add the mushrooms. Transfer the pot to the oven and braise until a sharp, thin-bladed knife inserted to the bone reveals no red within and only the faintest trace of pink, if any, about 25 minutes for the breast pieces, 40 minutes for the others. As the pieces are done, remove them from the pot and transfer them to a baking sheet.

5. Use tongs or a slotted spoon to transfer the mushrooms to a plate and set aside. Return the pot to the stovetop and reduce the liquid over high heat for 5 minutes, skimming any scum that rises to the surface. While the sauce is reducing, reheat the chicken pieces in the oven for 2 minutes. Off the heat, swirl the butter into the sauce, if using.

6. To serve, place 1 chicken piece on each of 8 warm dinner plates, and top with some mushrooms and sauce.

Chicken in Red Wine Sauce

■ *Serves 4* ■

Coq au vin, or chicken in red wine sauce, is a French bistro staple that is famously easy to prepare. You just empty a bottle or two of wine over some chicken, let it marinate, and then cook it. But this version tweaks the traditional recipe in a few important ways: the braising liquid is a more mightily seasoned concoction than you'll find in most recipes for *coq au vin,* and I add dried porcini mushrooms to the mix. If over-reduced, red wine becomes unpalatably concentrated and syrupy; the addition of distilled white vinegar here lightens up the marinade with some extra acidity and makes reducing the wine a more forgiving prospect.

Like any good bistro classic, this is delicious with Potato Gratin (page 222).

One 3½-pound chicken, cut into
    8 pieces
1 large Spanish onion, peeled and cut
    into 8 wedges
1 large carrot, peeled and cut on the
    bias into 1-inch pieces
12 cloves garlic, peeled and halved
    lengthwise
1 bottle (750 ml) full-bodied red wine
4 plum tomatoes, cut crosswise into
    1-inch rounds
Coarse salt
Freshly ground black pepper

Sugar
All-purpose flour, for dredging
1 cup olive oil or vegetable oil
3 tablespoons tomato paste
1 cup store-bought, reduced-sodium
    chicken broth or homemade
    Chicken Stock (page 244)
¼ cup distilled white vinegar (page 246)
¼ cup dried porcini mushrooms
    (page 243), rinsed
1 tablespoon chopped fresh thyme
    leaves
2 bay leaves

1. Wash the chicken pieces in cold running water and pat thoroughly dry with paper towels. Put the chicken pieces in a deep container just large enough to hold them in a single layer. Scatter the onion, carrot, and garlic over them. Pour in the red wine. Cover and let marinate in the refrigerator for 4 hours, or overnight.

2. About 30 minutes before you want to cook, put the tomatoes in a bowl and season with salt, pepper, and a pinch of sugar. Give a good toss and set aside at room temperature.

3. Remove the chicken from the refrigerator. Use tongs or a slotted spoon to transfer the chicken pieces to a plate and set aside. Pour the liquid and vegetables into a fine-mesh strainer set over a bowl; reserve them separately. Let all of the ingredients come to room temperature, about 20 minutes.

4. Preheat the oven to 325°F. Pat the chicken pieces dry with paper towels. Season the chicken pieces with salt and pepper, then dredge them in flour, shaking off any excess. Set aside.

5. In an ovenproof pot large enough to hold the chicken pieces in a single layer, heat the oil over medium-high heat until hot but not smoking. Add the chicken pieces and cook them on each side until the skin is nicely browned and some fat has been rendered, 4 to 5 minutes on each side. Transfer the chicken to a plate and set aside.

6. Discard all but 2 tablespoons of fat from the pot. Add the reserved vegetables and cook over medium-high heat, stirring occasionally, until lightly browned, about 10 minutes.

7. Stir in the tomato paste, then add the reserved red wine marinade, the chicken broth, white vinegar, dried porcini, thyme, bay leaves, 1½ tablespoons salt, and 1 teaspoon black pepper. Stir to integrate the ingredients. Bring to a boil over high heat.

8. Return the chicken pieces to the pot, cover, and braise in the oven until a sharp, thin-bladed knife inserted to the bone reveals no red within and only the faintest trace of pink, if any, about 25 minutes for the breast pieces, 40 minutes for the others. As the pieces are done, remove them from the pot and arrange them decoratively on a platter. Cover them with aluminum foil to keep them warm.

9. Strain the sauce and discard the vegetables. Return the sauce to the pot over high heat and let it reduce for 5 minutes, skimming off and discarding any fat that rises to the surface. If not serving immediately, let cool, cover, and refrigerate the chicken and sauce separately for a few days, but do not freeze. Reheat separately before proceeding.

10. To serve, spoon some sauce over the chicken pieces and pass any extra sauce alongside in a sauceboat.

Slow-Cooked Chicken in a Pot

■ Serves 4 ■

The French *poule au pot,* known to Americans by the far-less-poetic "chicken in a pot," is a one-pot marvel in which chicken pieces and a variety of vegetables are steamed in liquid and flavored by herbs. In my version, you first brown a whole chicken in butter, then stew it in a liquid flavored with vermouth and lots of garlic. While it cooks, the bird becomes very juicy and takes on all the nuances of the other ingredients.

Working with a whole chicken can get messy, so use the widest-mouthed pot available for ease of movement (make sure it has a cover), and have a good, sturdy set of tongs on hand for manipulating the bird.

One 3-pound chicken	4 tablespoons unsalted butter
Coarse salt	⅓ cup olive oil
Freshly ground black pepper	1 cup dry vermouth
10 sprigs assorted herbs (such as marjoram and thyme), plus 10 sprigs thyme	1 cup store-bought, reduced-sodium chicken broth or homemade Chicken Stock (page 244)
2 heads garlic, separated, half the cloves smashed and peeled, the other half left whole and unpeeled	1 tablespoon extra-virgin olive oil ½ large, or 1 small, Spanish onion, peeled and cut into 6 wedges
1 bay leaf	6 small new potatoes, quartered

1. Preheat the oven to 425°F. Wash the chicken under cold running water and pat dry with paper towels. Season the chicken inside and out with salt and pepper. Stuff the chicken cavity with the 10 herb sprigs, the smashed garlic, and the bay leaf. Tie the legs together with kitchen twine.

2. Set a heavy-bottomed ovenproof pot over medium-high heat, letting it get nice and hot. Add the butter and oil and cook until the butter melts and turns brown. Add the chicken and brown it all over, 3 to 4 minutes per side. Remove the chicken from the pot and set it aside on a platter.

3. Discard the fat from the pot, add the vermouth and thyme, and bring to a boil, scraping up any browned bits stuck on the bottom of the pot. Once the vermouth has almost evaporated, add the broth, extra-virgin olive oil, onion, unpeeled garlic, and a pinch of salt and pepper. Stir and cook for 1 minute. Return the chicken to the pot on top of the vegetables, scatter the quartered potatoes around it, and season them with salt and pepper.

4. Cover the pot and place it in the oven. Cook for 30 minutes, gently shaking the pot to move the vegetables around every 10 minutes or so. Remove the cover and let cook for another 15 to 20 minutes, until a sharp, thin-bladed knife inserted near the thighbone reveals no red within and only the faintest trace of pink, if any. Remove the pot from the oven.

5. To serve, transfer the chicken to a warm platter, snip off the string, and discard the herbs and garlic inside. Arrange the vegetables all around the chicken. Strain the sauce, spoon off any fat from the top, and pass it alongside the chicken and vegetables.

Steamed Whole Chicken with Three Variations

■ *Serves 4* ■

This is the purest example of one-pot cooking I can think of. It requires little more than a chicken and an inch of water. Amazingly, this produces a succulent, juicy chicken rather than a stringy, dried-out one. Equally pleasing is the liquid you're left with, a broth intensely flavored by the drippings from the bird that can be used as a stock for soups and sauces.

Organic, farm-raised chicken is so plentiful these days and readily available even at supermarkets that I urge you to use it for all of your poultry pursuits. But I especially recommend it for this recipe because the cooking technique can only bring out as much flavor and texture as the bird inherently possesses.

Serve this chicken with the broth on the side and a selection of seasonings and garnishes such as sea salt, ground pepper, whole-grain mustard, or Mustard Mayonnaise (page 231). This is a great recipe to make if you enjoy having a precooked meal on tap in the fridge.

One 3- to 4-pound chicken	**5 sprigs thyme**
Coarse salt	**1 lemon, halved**
Freshly ground black pepper	**7 cloves garlic, smashed and peeled**

1. Fill a large pot or stockpot with an inch or two of water. Set over medium heat and bring to a simmer.

2. Meanwhile, wash the chicken under cold running water and pat dry with paper towels. Season the chicken inside and out with salt and pepper. Stuff the cavity with the thyme sprigs, lemon halves, and garlic. Tie the legs together with kitchen twine.

3. Place the chicken in a steamer basket and set over the simmering water. Cover and steam for 45 minutes to 1 hour, until the skin is taut and the bird is plump all over. To ensure doneness, be sure that a sharp, thin-bladed knife inserted at the thigh-bone reveals no red within and only the faintest trace of pink, if any.

4. Transfer the chicken to a cutting board. Snip off and discard the kitchen string. Discard the lemon, thyme, and garlic. When you have a chance, strain the broth and let it cool. Refrigerate it for 2 to 3 days or freeze for up to a month for use in soups and stews. If not serving the chicken immediately, let cool, cover, and refrigerate for a few days. Reheat before proceeding, unless you prefer to enjoy the chicken cold.

5. To serve, carve the chicken and present it with a selection of seasonings and garnishes (see Headnote).

VARIATIONS

Moroccan Chicken

Season the chicken with ground cumin and coriander, two spices used in North African cuisine. After removing the chicken from the pot, skim any fat from the surface of the liquid. Put 1 cup couscous in a bowl and add enough of the liquid just to cover, cover with plastic wrap, and let sit for 5 minutes. Fluff with a fork and serve alongside the chicken.

Tomato-Steamed Chicken

Add 2 chopped tomatoes, 1 crushed garlic clove, a few sprigs of fresh thyme, and a splash of white wine to the water in the bottom of the pot before adding the chicken. Be sure to discard the thyme before serving. Reserve the broth for use as a simple soup with orzo (page 217).

Asian-Style Steamed Chicken

Add 2 cloves sliced garlic, 1 tablespoon grated ginger, a few tablespoons of soy sauce, and a splash of rice wine vinegar to the water before adding the chicken to the pot. Strain the broth after removing the chicken and discard the solids. Reserve the broth for use as a soup—you can quickly cook capellini (page 216) in it and add chopped pieces of chicken, or save it for another day.

Duck with Dried Fruits

■ *Serves 4* ■

This recipe avoids the daunting task of roasting a whole duck by first quartering the bird, which allows every piece of skin to come into direct contact with a hot surface while cooking, guaranteeing the crispy, crunchy effect that everyone loves. A dark-meat game bird, duck is one of the quintessential fall ingredients. Its rich skin demands something sweet to offset it, and in the autumn, when most fresh fruits aren't in season, dried fruits are the way to go.

This dish cries out for an accompaniment of Wild Rice (page 213).

One 4-pound duck, quartered	¾ cup dried apricots, cut into
Coarse salt	½-inch dice
Freshly ground black pepper	¾ cup dried currants
1 cup dry white wine	2 tablespoons orange juice
¾ cup water	1 teaspoon sugar
1½ teaspoons distilled white vinegar	Pinch of ground nutmeg
(page 246)	Pinch of ground allspice
¾ cup golden raisins	Pinch of ground mace
¾ cup dried cranberries	

1. Preheat the oven to 350°F. Wash the duck pieces under cold running water and pat dry with paper towels. Season the duck pieces all over with salt and pepper.

2. Put the duck pieces skin side down in a wide, deep ovenproof pot and cook slowly over low heat, rendering the fat, for about 10 minutes, pouring off the fat periodically as it collects in the pot.

3. Turn the duck pieces and transfer the pot to the oven. Roast for 35 to 40 minutes, until the duck is firm and darkly browned and the juices run clear when the pieces are pierced with a sharp, thin-bladed knife. Remove from the oven, transfer the duck pieces to a large plate, cover with aluminum foil to keep them warm, and set aside.

4. Pour off and discard the fat from the pot. Pour in the wine, bring to a boil over medium-high heat, and stir, scraping up any browned bits stuck to the bottom of the pot. Add the water, vinegar, raisins, cranberries, apricots, currants, orange juice, sugar, 1 teaspoon salt, a pinch of black pepper, the nutmeg, allspice, and mace. Cover and cook at a low simmer until the sauce is nicely thickened and the flavors are concentrated, 10 to 15 minutes. Return the duck to the pan for a few minutes to reheat it.

5. To serve, transfer 1 duck piece to each of 4 warm plates, and spoon some sauce and dried fruits on top.

Mushroom-Poached Squab

Serves 4

This recipe isn't particularly difficult, but it is one of the most involved in the book because it requires advance preparation (the squab have to be seasoned 12 hours ahead) and careful monitoring of the cooking-liquid temperature (you will need a kitchen thermometer). All that said, if you or someone dear to you loves game bird in season, this is a real one-of-a-kind treat.

Serve this with pastina (page 217), which can be cooked in the broth after the squab have been removed, or precooked orzo or tubetti (page 217), placing them in individual bowls and ladling the hot broth on top.

4 squab (approximately 12 ounces each)
Coarse salt
Freshly ground black pepper
2 tablespoons unsalted butter
2 tablespoons plus 1 teaspoon olive oil
24 pearl onions, halved, or cippoline onions cut into thirds or quarters, depending on size
24 small white mushrooms, or 12 larger ones, cut into ½-inch slices
3 cloves garlic, peeled and thinly sliced
1 large carrot, peeled and cut into small dice
1 large Spanish onion, peeled and cut into small dice

2 stalks celery, cut into small dice
1½ cups dried porcini mushrooms (page 243), rinsed
1 cup dry white wine
1½ teaspoons distilled white vinegar (page 246)
1 tablespoon chopped fresh thyme leaves
2 bay leaves
2½ quarts hot water
2 tablespoons chopped fresh flat-leaf parsley leaves
Truffle oil or shaved black truffle, optional

1. Pat the squab dry inside and out. Season the squab inside and out with salt and pepper and refrigerate for at least 12 hours to dry out the bird.

2. When ready to proceed, melt the butter with 1 teaspoon of the olive oil in a heavy-bottomed pot set over low heat. Add the pearl onions and cook for 3 to 4 minutes, then add the mushrooms and garlic. Season with ½ teaspoon salt and ¼ teaspoon black pepper. Cook, stirring occasionally, without letting the mushrooms or onions brown, for 7 to 8 minutes. Remove the mushrooms and pearl onions from the pot and set aside on a plate.

3. Add the remaining 2 tablespoons olive oil to the pan, along with the carrot, onion, and celery, raise the heat to medium, and cook the vegetables for 3 to 4 minutes. Add the porcini mushrooms and stir to coat them with the oil. Add the white wine, bring to a boil over high heat, and cook, scraping any flavorful bits off the bottom of the pot.

4. When the wine has evaporated, add the vinegar, thyme, and bay leaves. Stir and add the hot water, 2 tablespoons plus 1 teaspoon salt, and ½ teaspoon black pepper. Bring to a boil, and skim off any scum that rises to the surface. Lower the heat and simmer until the liquid becomes very flavorful, 25 to 30 minutes.

5. While the liquid is simmering, remove the squab from the refrigerator and bring to room temperature.

6. Insert a kitchen thermometer in the liquid to ensure that the temperature stays at 190°F, adjusting the level of heat if necessary. Immerse the squabs in the liquid, with the breast facing down and the legs facing up. Cook for 5 minutes, then turn the birds over and cook for an additional 5 to 7 minutes for rare, 10 to 13 minutes for medium-rare. The squab are done when the skin feels firm and the legs spring back in place if you bend them back from the body.

7. Remove the squabs from the pot, transfer them to a cutting board, and cover with aluminum foil to keep them warm.

8. Bring the cooking liquid to a boil over high heat and skim any fat or scum that rises to the surface to purify the flavor and appearance of the sauce.

9. To serve, divide the mushrooms and onions among 4 wide, shallow bowls. Place 1 squab in each of the bowls and spoon some broth over each serving. Garnish with chopped parsley. If desired, finish with a drizzle of truffle oil or top with sliced fresh truffle.

Mushroom-Poached Poussin or Cornish Game Hen

This recipe also works well for poussin (12 to 14 ounces each) if you increase the cooking time to 24 to 26 minutes, or for Cornish game hen if you increase the cooking time to 20 to 22 minutes.

TOMORROW'S TABLE

The cooking liquid can be strained and used to add an exceptional depth of flavor to soups and stews centered around mushrooms such as Mushroom, Barley, and Sage Soup (page 32) and Mushroom Stew (page 80). Use it in place of all or part of the stock called for in the recipe.

Moroccan-Spice-Braised Lamb Shanks

Serves 6

The lamb shank is to me what "Piano Man" is to Billy Joel—my first claim-to-fame; the one everyone requests; the dish I'll be cooking in the afterlife at that big benefit event up in the sky. The robust dish I've served in restaurants for almost fifteen years gets its signature flavor from the strategic use of distilled white vinegar and anchovy. The former lightens up the overall character of the dish; the latter punches up the other flavors including that of the lamb itself.

In this version, I use the long, slow braising technique to infuse lamb—a popular meat in North African cuisine—with some of the flavors it goes best with, including the Moroccan spices cumin, coriander, cinnamon, and paprika. Serve this with harissa (see the note at the end of the recipe) and couscous (page 208) or millet (page 209).

6 lamb foreshanks (about 1¼ pounds each)
Coarse salt
Freshly ground black pepper
½ cup olive oil
2 stalks celery, coarsely chopped
1 medium carrot, peeled and coarsely chopped
1 large Spanish onion, peeled and coarsely chopped
2 heaping tablespoons tomato paste
3 plum tomatoes, coarsely chopped
3 sprigs marjoram
2 bay leaves
1 tablespoon green peppercorns, packed in brine, rinsed and drained

1 anchovy fillet, rinsed and patted dry
3 whole heads garlic, cut in half crosswise
2 cups dry white wine
⅓ cup distilled white vinegar (page 246)
1 teaspoon sugar
5 cups store-bought, reduced-sodium chicken broth or homemade Chicken Stock (page 244)
2 cups water
1 tablespoon ground coriander
1 tablespoon sweet paprika
2 teaspoons ground cumin
½ teaspoon cayenne pepper
½ teaspoon cinnamon

1. Preheat the oven to 325°F. Season the lamb shanks liberally with salt and pepper. With a sharp knife, aiming about 1 inch from the bottom (narrow end) of the shank bones, cut through the meat and tendon, down to the bone and all the way around; this will help the meat to plump up attractively when cooked. Set aside.

2. Heat the olive oil in a roasting pan over medium-high heat. Add the shanks and brown them all over, 3 to 4 minutes per side. Transfer to a plate and set aside. Pour off all put 2 tablespoons of fat from the pan.

3. Add the celery, carrot, and onion to the pan and cook over medium heat until very soft, 8 to 10 minutes. Add the tomato paste, stirring well to coat the vegetables, and cook for 1 to 2 minutes. Add the tomatoes, stir, and cook for 3 minutes.

4. Add the marjoram, bay leaves, peppercorns, anchovy, and garlic and cook for 2 to 3 minutes. Add the white wine, vinegar, and sugar and bring to a boil over high heat. Add the chicken broth, water, coriander, paprika, cumin, cayenne, and cinnamon. Stir well and return to the boil.

5. Return the shanks to the roasting pan. Cover with aluminum foil, transfer to the oven and braise for 1 hour. Remove the foil and braise for 3 more hours, turning the shanks over every half hour, until the meat is very tender. If not serving immediately, let cool, cover, and refrigerate for a few days or freeze for up to 1 month. Reheat before proceeding.

6. Remove the shanks from the braising liquid and set aside on a plate, covered with aluminum foil to keep them warm. Strain the liquid into a bowl and let it rest for a few minutes. Use a large spoon to skim off any fat that rises to the surface.

7. To serve, place a shank on each of 6 warm dinner plates or wide, shallow bowls and spoon some braising liquid on top.

TOMORROW'S TABLE

If you have any remaining shanks, bone them, shred the meat, and refrigerate it in the braising liquid. Reheat and serve over couscous (page 208) for a quick lunch.

HARISSA

Harissa is a fiery Tunisian condiment made from hot peppers and tomatoes and is used to flavor everything from couscous to pastas to sandwiches. It is available in cans at Middle Eastern markets and many gourmet shops. You can also order it online (see Mail-Order Sources, page 247).

Seven-Hour Leg of Lamb

■ *Serves 6* ■

My recipe for leg of lamb calls for studding the lamb with garlic, seasoning it assertively with salt and pepper, and loading it up with lots of rosemary and thyme. After that, the key to the success of this lamb is to baste the meat as frequently as possible with the pan drippings. Because the lamb is cooking in a minimum of liquid—just enough to keep it from drying out—this will produce a crusty exterior and supple, falling-apart meat within.

You should be able to buy the leg of lamb tied, but if not, you can easily do this at home. Roll the meat carefully into a tight roll with as uniform a thickness as possible. Tie the meat with kitchen string every few inches—as you would a roast—securing it firmly to maintain an even thickness from end to end.

Serve this with Potato Gratin (page 222).

One 7-to-8 pound boneless leg of
    lamb, rolled and tied
10 cloves garlic, peeled and cut into
    thin slivers plus 4 whole heads
    garlic, cut in half crosswise
Coarse salt
Freshly ground black pepper
1 cup olive oil

1 bottle (750 ml) dry white wine
2 large Spanish onions, peeled and
    halved
2 large carrots, peeled and cut on a
    bias into 4 pieces each
10 sprigs rosemary
10 sprigs thyme

1. Preheat the oven to 300°F. Using a sharp, thin-bladed knife, make small ½-inch-thick slits all over the lamb. Slide a garlic sliver into each slit using the edge of the knife. Season the lamb all over with salt and pepper.

2. In a roasting pan large enough to hold the leg of lamb comfortably, heat the oil over medium-high heat until hot but not smoking. Add the lamb and brown on all sides, 3 to 4 minutes per side. Remove the lamb and set aside.

3. Discard all but 2 tablespoons of fat from the pan. Add the halved garlic heads, white wine, onions, carrots, rosemary, and thyme and cook, stirring, until the vegetables begin to soften, 3 to 4 minutes.

4. Return the lamb to the pan, cover with aluminum foil, and transfer to the oven. Roast, basting every 20 to 30 minutes with the pan juices, for 7 hours. Remove from the oven, transfer the roast to a cutting board, cover with aluminum foil, and let rest for 10 minutes.

5. Snip off and discard the strings and carve the leg crosswise into individual servings. Serve family-style from a platter or divide among individual plates.

VARIATION

Garlic Leg of Lamb

For a pronounced garlic flavor, line the leg with whole, peeled cloves from 1 head of garlic before rolling it up. The garlic roasts along with the leg and is soft and mellow tasting when the lamb is done.

"Regular" Leg of Lamb

If you don't have 7 hours to make this dish, roast a leg of lamb in about 2½ hours by raising the oven temperature to 325°F and roasting the lamb *uncovered* until an instant-read thermometer inserted to the center reads 125°F for rare, 140°F for medium. You won't get the same, wonderfully crusty exterior, but it is still delicious.

TOMORROW'S TABLE

If you have leftover meat, shred it and make a soup by adding store-bought, reduced-sodium beef broth and cooked tubetti (page 217).

Classic Braised Beef Brisket

■ *Serves 8* ■

There are few dishes as perfectly suited to Sunday dinner as a classic, braised beef brisket. For someone like me, it's an especially welcome treat because it's rarely served in restaurants, even mine, so I've only enjoyed it at home. Brisket is a cut from just below the steer's shoulder and must be cooked slowly to break down all of its connective tissue. Patience pays great dividends: Even if you are only cooking for two or four people, make all 4 pounds recommended here and use the leftovers for a week's worth of sandwiches.

One 4-pound beef brisket
Garlic powder
Freshly ground black pepper
Coarse salt
¼ cup olive oil
1 large carrot, peeled and cut into small dice
1 large Spanish onion, peeled and cut into small dice
1 stalk celery, cut into small dice
2 cloves garlic, smashed and peeled

¼ cup tomato paste
1 teaspoon sugar
2 cups red wine
5 tablespoons distilled white vinegar (page 246)
4 cups store-bought, reduced-sodium beef broth
4 sprigs thyme
2 bay leaves
1 tablespoon black peppercorns

1. Two to 3 hours before you want to cook the brisket, season it generously all over with garlic powder, pepper, and a little salt. Cover and let marinate in the refrigerator.

2. Preheat the oven to 325°F.

3. Heat the oil in a roasting pan over medium-high heat until hot but not smoking. Add the brisket and brown it on both sides, about 5 minutes per side. (Don't be afraid to let it develop a dark, hard, seared crust.) Transfer the brisket to a large plate or platter and set aside.

4. Add the carrot, onion, celery, and garlic to the pan, scraping up any browned bits stuck to the bottom. Season with salt and pepper, and cook, stirring, until the vegetables are softened and nicely browned, about 12 minutes.

5. Add the tomato paste and sugar and stir well to coat all the vegetables. Continue to cook, stirring, for 2 to 3 minutes. Stir in the red wine and vinegar and bring to a boil.

6. Return the brisket to the pan, skin side up. Add the beef broth, thyme, bay leaves, peppercorns, and 1 tablespoon salt and bring to a boil over high heat, then cover and transfer to the oven. Braise until the brisket is fork-tender, 3 to 3½ hours. During this long, slow process, it's okay if the very top of the brisket pokes out of the liquid, but if the liquid level drops much further, add some hot water to the pan.

7. Remove the pan from the oven, transfer the brisket to a cutting board, cover with aluminum foil to keep warm, and let rest for 5 minutes.

8. Meanwhile, strain the sauce into a medium saucepan, bring to a boil, and skim any scum that rises to the surface.

9. To serve, cut the brisket into thin slices against the grain and arrange on a platter, passing the sauce alongside.

Mushroom-Braised Short Ribs

Serves 6

When you experience a craving for beef, nothing satisfies like short ribs, which have as pure and true a beef flavor as you could imagine. This intensity derives from a number of factors including their dense consistency, their relatively high fat content, and the fact that they are affixed to a bone, which is also a source of tremendous flavor.

One of the most impressive things about short ribs is that they have the ability to take on the flavors of other ingredients during slow cooking without sacrificing their own beefy flavor. Here, they are paired with dried morel mushrooms, to create a potent double whammy of the most extreme examples of beef and mushroom known to man.

When I make this at home, I serve it with Mashed Potatoes (page 221) or Potato Gratin (page 222).

6 pounds short ribs (about 6 pieces)	8 cloves garlic, smashed and peeled
Coarse salt	2 cups dry white wine
Freshly ground black pepper	⅓ cup distilled white vinegar (page 246)
Garlic powder	9 cups store-bought, reduced-sodium
¼ cup olive oil	beef broth
1 medium Spanish onion, peeled and	3 sprigs thyme
coarsely chopped	1 bay leaf
3 stalks celery, coarsely chopped	1 cup dried morel or porcini
1 carrot, peeled and coarsely chopped	mushrooms (page 243), rinsed

1. The day before cooking, season the ribs with salt, pepper, and garlic powder. Cover with plastic wrap and refrigerate overnight.

2. Preheat the oven to 325°F.

3. Heat the olive oil in a roasting pan over medium-high heat until hot but not smoking. Add the ribs and brown them on all sides, about 1 minute per side. Remove from the pan and set aside.

4. Discard all but 2 tablespoons fat from the pan. Add the onion, celery, carrot, and garlic to the pan. Cook, stirring often, until lightly browned, about 8 minutes. Add the wine, vinegar, broth, thyme, and bay leaf. Stir in the mushrooms. Bring to a boil over high heat.

5. Return the ribs to the pan, cover with aluminum foil, and braise in the oven for 1 hour. Remove the aluminum foil and cook for 3 more hours or until the meat is very tender and falling off the bone.

6. To serve, remove the ribs from the braising liquid and divide them among 6 warm, shallow bowls. (Leave the bone—it makes a dramatic presentation.) Strain the braising liquid, discarding the solids. Skim off and discard the fat from the liquid and pass as a sauce at the table.

VARIATION

Beer-Braised Short Ribs

Bring one of the most perfect accompaniments to beef—beer—to short ribs. Replace the wine with beer and omit the vinegar and morels. The success of this variation depends on the right beer: You want a dark or honey brown-colored brew, something with an inherent sweetness and no bitterness whatsoever.

Grilled Short Rib and Horseradish Sandwich

Let the short ribs cool, then remove the meat from the bone and cut it into 1-inch-thick slices. Swirl some grated horseradish into the braising liquid. Grill the short-rib slices on one side over a high heat until caramelized and nice grill marks have formed, then turn and cook on the other side. Or sear them in a sauté pan with 2 tablespoons olive oil over high heat. Sandwich between slices of your favorite bread and dress with some of the horseradish-infused braising liquid.

Beef on a String Soup and Sandwich

■ *Serves 8* ■

This may seem like an unusual way to make soup and a sandwich, but it's actually founded on French culinary tradition. *Boeuf à la ficelle* (beef on a string) cooks beef by tying it with string and lowering the meat into a pot of broth, turning the meat meltingly tender. The basic principle is the same here: The meat is lowered into a cauldron of hot liquid, which cooks it, while the meat flavors the broth at the same time. Only here, the cooking liquid itself becomes a soup with the addition of pasta and the beef becomes the centerpiece of a make-your-own-sandwich spread.

4 filets mignons (about 12 ounces each)
Coarse salt
Freshly ground black pepper
2 tablespoons olive oil
2 small carrots, peeled and cut on the bias into 1-inch pieces
2 stalks celery, peeled and cut on the bias into 1-inch pieces
1 large onion, peeled and cut into large dice
¼ cup dried porcini mushrooms (page 243), rinsed

1 clove garlic, peeled and minced
2½ quarts water
Splash dry white wine
A few drops distilled white vinegar (page 246)
2 bay leaves
Pinch of sugar
½ pound pastina (page 217) or other rice-sized pasta
Cornichons, horseradish, and Mustard Mayonnaise (page 231), for serving
Sliced white bread, for making sandwiches

1. Season the filets mignons with salt and pepper. Tie each filet around its equator with kitchen string, leaving about a foot of excess string. Find a spare wooden kitchen spoon long enough to rest across the top of a large, heavy-bottomed pot. Tie the end of each string to the spoon so that the filets can be lowered into and raised from the pot easily.

2. Heat the olive oil in the pot over medium-high heat until hot but not smoking.

Add the carrots, celery, onion, porcini, and garlic. Stir and cook for 15 minutes, until the vegetables soften but do not brown.

3. Add the water, white wine, white vinegar, bay leaves, sugar, and 3½ tablespoons salt. Bring to a boil over high heat.

4. Lower the filets into the pot, resting the wooden spoon across the top. Simmer for 12 to 14 minutes for medium-rare, or longer if using larger cuts of beef (or if you like your beef more well done). Check for doneness by cutting into the center of 1 piece with a sharp, thin-bladed knife. For rare or medium-rare, it should be pink at the outsides and red toward the center, but warmed all the way through. As it becomes more well done, it will be less red and more pink throughout.

5. Remove the filets from the pot, cut off and discard the strings, and transfer the meat to a cutting board. Cover with aluminum foil and let rest while you finish the soup.

6. Add the pastina to the pot and cook until al dente, following the time guidelines on the package. (If using millet, precook it following the instructions on page 209.)

7. To serve, slice the beef against the grain, arrange on a platter, and serve with cornichons, horseradish, mayonnaise, or other desired condiments and sliced bread for sandwich-making. Ladle some soup into each of 4 warm bowls and serve alongside.

Florentine Pot Roast with Red Wine, Mushrooms, and Tomatoes

■ *Serves 6* ■

Pot roast offers a fascinating look at the differences between home cooking in the United States and Europe. This dish, which to us is a way to cook such staples as carrots, onions, and potatoes, is to Europeans an opportunity to enjoy their most tried-and-true ingredients. This recipe is based on the Italian *stracotto,* which means "slow cooked." It's a favorite wintertime preparation in Florence and the small Tuscan hill towns that surround it. This version uses an all-star lineup of the region's ingredients, including red wine, dried porcini, and canned tomatoes. Not surprisingly, this pot roast is excellent with its compatriot accompaniment, Polenta (page 210).

One 2½-pound eye of the round roast, excess fat trimmed, tied with kitchen string at 1-inch intervals
3 cloves garlic, peeled and cut into thin slivers, plus 2 cloves smashed and peeled
Coarse salt
Freshly ground black pepper
½ cup olive oil
½ pound slab bacon (page 241), cut into ½-inch strips
2 medium Spanish onions, peeled and quartered
2 celery stalks, cut crosswise into ¼-inch pieces

1 large carrot, peeled and cut into ¼-inch rounds
¼ cup tomato paste
Pinch of sugar
2 cups red wine, plus more if needed
1 cup water or store-bought, reduced-sodium beef broth
1 cup dried porcini mushrooms (page 243), rinsed
One 28-ounce can plum tomatoes from Italy, drained of liquid and squeezed by hand to remove excess moisture
Handful fresh oregano leaves

1. Preheat the oven to 300°F. Using a sharp, thin-bladed knife, make small, ½-inch-deep slits all over the beef. Slide a garlic sliver into each slit using the edge of the knife. Season the beef generously with salt and pepper.

2. Heat the oil in a large, heavy-bottomed ovenproof pot over medium-high heat until hot but not smoking. Add the beef and sear it well on all sides until well browned, about 4 minutes per side. (Tongs are a good tool for turning the meat.) Transfer the beef to a plate and set it aside.

3. Pour off all but 2 tablespoons of fat from the pot. Add the bacon, onions, celery, and carrot and cook over medium-high heat, stirring, until the vegetables begin to soften, about 5 minutes. Add the tomato paste and sugar and stir to coat the other ingredients. Add the wine and water, raise the heat to high, and boil until the liquid has reduced by half, about 5 minutes. Add the mushrooms, tomatoes, and oregano and season lightly with salt and pepper, keeping in mind that the bacon is salty.

4. Return the beef to the pot. It should be half to three-quarters covered by the liquid. If it is not, add some more wine, water, or broth. Bring to a boil over high heat. Cover the pot, transfer it to the oven, and braise the beef for 2½ to 3 hours, turning the beef over and giving the liquid a stir every half hour. Make sure that the liquid is simmering gently; if it's bubbling aggressively, reduce the oven temperature to 275°F. When done, the meat will be firm to the touch and pink at the center. If not serving immediately, let cool, cover, and refrigerate for a few days or freeze for up to 1 month. Reheat before proceeding.

5. To serve, transfer the beef to a cutting board and slice it against the grain into 6 pieces. Place 1 slice on each of 6 warm dinner plates. Spoon some sauce over each serving and pass extra sauce on the side in a sauceboat.

TOMORROW'S TABLE

Pappardelle alla Stracotto

To make a meaty pasta sauce, coarsely chop any leftover beef and refrigerate it separately from the sauce. The next day, spoon off and discard any fat that has risen to the top of the sauce. Reheat the sauce gently in a pot set over low heat. If desired, blend with an immersion blender for a few seconds to chop the vegetables. Return the beef to the sauce and toss with hot pasta such as pappardelle (page 219), egg noodles (page 217), or fettuccine (page 219).

Braised Oxtail with Cipolline Onions

■ Serves 6 ■

Generations ago, oxtail was enormously popular as the centerpiece of stews and as an economical way to infuse soups with great, beefy flavor. For some reason, it fell out of fashion for a long time, but has resurfaced in contemporary restaurants where new generations of diners have discovered its rich flavor.

I've always loved oxtail because it's so well suited to my penchant for slow cooking. In fact, there simply are no oxtail dishes that aren't slow cooked. The meat takes a long time to break down and release all of its fat, which must be removed before serving. Serve this dish with something that will soak up the savory sauce, such as Mashed Potatoes (page 221) or egg noodles (page 217).

By the way, most of what goes by the name oxtail today actually comes from a cow.

6 oxtails (about 1 pound each)
Coarse salt
Freshly ground black pepper
Garlic powder
¼ cup olive oil
¼ cup fresh marjoram, thyme, or
    oregano leaves
¼ cup fresh rosemary leaves
1 large carrot, peeled and cut into
    small dice
1 medium Spanish onion, peeled and
    cut into fine dice

2 stalks celery, cut into small dice
3 cloves garlic, peeled and minced
¼ cup tomato paste
Pinch of sugar
4 cups robust red wine such as Shiraz
    or Zinfandel
2 quarts store-bought, reduced-
    sodium beef broth
1 bay leaf
12 ounces medium cipolline onions
    (about 2 cups), peeled
2 tablespoons whole-grain mustard

1. Preheat the oven to 325°F. Season the meat all over with salt, pepper, and garlic powder.

2. Heat the oil in a large, heavy-bottomed pot over medium-high heat until hot but not smoking. Add the oxtail pieces, working in batches if necessary, and brown on all sides, 3 to 4 minutes per side. Transfer the oxtail to a plate and set aside.

3. Pour off all but 2 tablespoons of the fat from the pot. Add the carrot, onion, celery, and garlic. Reduce the heat to medium and cook the vegetables for 5 to 10 minutes, stirring occasionally, until softened. Add the tomato paste and sugar and stir to coat the other ingredients with the paste.

4. Stir in the wine, broth, and bay leaf. Scrape up any browned bits from the bottom of the pot and bring the liquid to a boil over high heat. Return the meat to the pot.

5. Reduce the heat until the liquid is just simmering, cover the pot, and braise in the oven for 1 hour. Remove the cover and cook for 40 minutes. Add the cippoline onions and braise for 20 minutes longer, until the meat comes right off the bone with a gentle tug of a fork. If it is not yet tender, return it to the oven for another 15 minutes and test again.

6. Use tongs or a slotted spoon to transfer the oxtails to a plate; set aside. Pick out and discard the bay leaf. Skim any fat from the surface of the braising liquid and stir in the mustard. Taste and season with more salt and pepper if necessary. If not serving immediately, let cool, cover, and refrigerate for a few days or freeze for up to 1 month. Reheat before proceeding.

7. To serve, divide the oxtails and sauce among 6 plates.

CIPOLLINE ONIONS

These Italian onions are distinctly small and squat, with perhaps the sweetest flavor of any member of the onion family. If you cannot find them, pearl onions are a perfectly acceptable substitute.

Braised Beef Cheeks

■ *Serves 4* ■

Beef cheeks are just starting to find an audience here in the United States, but they're one of the most flavorful parts of the cow. (And of other creatures for that matter. When you cook a whole fish, make sure you don't leave the cheeks behind.) Like short ribs, they are richly gelatinous, full of natural flavor that permeates their cooking liquid when braised. Even after the fat has been removed from the resulting sauce, the flavor it leaves behind is unmistakable.

I can't talk (or write) about beef cheeks without thinking about my friend and fellow chef-in-arms Mario Batali. We have nicknames for each other based on our favorite cuts of meat. He calls me Shanks. I call him Beef Cheeks. I'm glad to have written this book if for no other reason than to have a public forum for setting the record straight as to why I've been calling him that all these years.

Unless you have access to a truly world-class butcher, you will need to special-order beef cheeks in advance, but they're worth the planning (see Mail-Order Sources, page 247). I don't suggest replacing them with any alternatives because they're really the reason for making this dish.

6 beef cheeks (6 to 8 ounces each)
Coarse salt
Freshly ground black pepper
Garlic powder
¼ cup plus 3 tablespoons olive oil
2 stalks celery, coarsely chopped
1 medium carrot, peeled and coarsely chopped
1 large Spanish onion, peeled and coarsely chopped
½ cup tomato paste
5 sprigs thyme

1 bay leaf
1 tablespoon whole black peppercorns
3 anchovy fillets, rinsed and patted dry
1 whole head garlic, cut in half crosswise
2 cups red wine
2 cups dry white wine
⅓ cup distilled white vinegar (page 246)
1 teaspoon sugar
3 cups store-bought, reduced-sodium chicken broth, homemade Chicken Stock (page 244), or water

1. The day before cooking, season the beef cheeks with salt, pepper, and garlic powder. Cover with plastic wrap and refrigerate overnight.

2. Preheat the oven to 325°F.

3. Heat ¼ cup of the oil in a roasting pan over medium-high heat until hot but not smoking. Add the cheeks to the pan and brown on both sides, about 2 minutes per side. Transfer the cheeks to a plate or platter and set aside.

4. Drain off and discard the fat from the pan. Add the remaining 3 tablespoons olive oil to the pan and set over medium-high heat. Add the celery, carrot, and onion and cook, stirring, until very soft but not browned, 7 to 8 minutes. Add the tomato paste and cook for 2 minutes, stirring to coat the vegetables. Add the thyme, bay leaf, peppercorns, anchovies, and garlic. Cook, stirring, for another 3 minutes.

5. Add the red and white wines, vinegar, and sugar, and bring to a boil over high heat. Pour in the broth and return to a boil.

6. Return the beef cheeks to the pan, immersing them in the liquid. Cover the roasting pan with aluminum foil and braise in the oven for 1 hour. Remove the foil and braise for 3 more hours or until the meat is very tender. If not serving immediately, let cool, cover, and refrigerate for a few days or freeze for up to 1 month. Reheat before proceeding.

7. To serve, remove the cheeks from the braising liquid and divide among 6 warm, shallow bowls. Strain the braising liquid, discarding the solids. Skim off and discard the fat from the liquid and pass the sauce separately at the table.

VARIATIONS

Beef Cheek Ravioli

Beef cheeks are rich and a little goes a long way. Accordingly, they make for an ideal ravioli filling. Coarsely chop the braised beef cheeks and mix with an equal volume of ricotta freshly grated Parmesan cheese, or a combination. Follow the instructions on page 220 to make and cook ravioli.

Braised Pork Shank

Pork shank is a dramatic cut from the enormous upper portion of the pig's leg, the same area from which ham is procured. (In fact, you *might* see it dubbed "fresh ham" or "leg butt half roast" in the supermarket. See also Mail-Order Sources, page 247.) Its girth is misleading; the meat within is actually relatively lean and, if cooked properly, quite succulent. This is a special-occasion kind of thing, more akin to a crown roast than to pork loin or shoulder. When the time comes to carve it, this impenetrable-looking mass might be intimidating, but you'll impress your friends (and yourself) when you discover how easy it actually is.

Two 3-to-4 pound pork shanks, bone in
Coarse salt
Freshly ground black pepper
2 cups olive oil
2 large carrots, peeled and cut on the
    bias into 2-inch segments
2 medium Spanish onions, peeled and
    quartered
2 stalks celery, cut on the bias into
    2-inch segments

12 cloves garlic, unpeeled
1 bottle (750 ml) dry white wine
⅔ cup distilled white vinegar
    (page 246)
1½ tablespoons mustard oil (available
    from Middle Eastern specialty
    shops and gourmet grocers; see
    also Mail-Order Sources, page 247)
1 tablespoon black peppercorns

1. Preheat the oven to 350°F. Season the shanks with salt and pepper.

2. Heat the oil in a large roasting pan over medium-high heat until hot but not smoking. Add the shanks and brown on all sides, about 8 minutes per side. Remove from the pan and set aside.

3. Pour off all but 2 tablespoons fat from the pan. Add the carrots, onions, celery, and garlic and cook over medium-high heat, stirring, until the vegetables are softened but not browned, about 5 minutes.

4. Add the wine, vinegar, mustard oil, and peppercorns and bring to a boil, stirring and scraping up any browned bits stuck to the bottom of the pan. Return the shanks to the pan, cover, and roast in the oven until the shanks attain an internal temperature of 150°F on an instant-read thermometer inserted in the center of the shank, about 3½ hours. Transfer the shanks to a cutting board, cover with aluminum foil to keep them warm, and let rest for 10 minutes. If not serving immediately, let cool, cover, and refrigerate for a few days or freeze for up to 1 month. Reheat before proceeding.

5. Strain the cooking liquid through a fine-mesh strainer set over a bowl. Discard the solids and let the sauce settle for 5 minutes, then spoon off any fat that has risen to the surface. If necessary, reheat gently in a pot over medium heat.

6. To carve the meat, secure it in place with a meat fork and slice from the thinner side of the shank. Then, turn the shank over onto the carved side. Cut slices perpendicular to the bone, then cut along the bone to remove the slices.

7. To serve, place slices of pork on 8 warm plates and top with some sauce.

Portuguese-Style Pork Roast
with Steamed Clams

■ *Serves 4* ■

One of my all-time favorite combinations of pork and shellfish is the Portuguese pairing of pork and clams, which are united in a number of that country's favorite dishes, including several stews featuring crumbled sausage or marinated pork cubes (e.g., *cataplana, stoccafisso, alentejana*). This recipe borrows inspiration from those classics, adapting them to my personal affection for roasted pork loin on the bone and cooking the clams in its tangy, slightly spicy sauce.

5 plum tomatoes, coarsely chopped
Coarse salt
Freshly ground black pepper
Sugar
One 4½-pound bone-in pork loin
  (about 4 or 5 chops)
4 cloves garlic, peeled and cut into
  thin slivers, plus 6 cloves garlic,
  peeled and halved
½ cup olive oil
1 large Spanish onion, peeled, halved,
  and thinly sliced

1 cup dry white wine
1 teaspoon fresh thyme leaves
1 teaspoon fresh marjoram or oregano
  leaves
Pinch of crushed red pepper
1¼ cups bottled clam juice
1½ pounds small clams (about
  24 clams), rinsed and scrubbed
  (page 49)
2 tablespoons chopped fresh flat-leaf
  parsley leaves

1. About 30 minutes before you want to cook, put the tomatoes in a bowl and season them with salt, pepper, and sugar. Set aside.

2. Preheat the oven to 425°F. Using a sharp, thin-bladed knife, make small ½-inch-deep slits all over the pork loin. Slide a garlic sliver into each slit using the edge of the knife. Season the pork all over with salt and pepper.

3. Heat the olive oil in a large, heavy-bottomed ovenproof pot over medium-high

heat. Add the pork and brown on all sides, about 4 minutes per side. Remove the pork from the pot and set aside.

4. Pour off all but 2 tablespoons of oil from the pot. Add the onion and halved garlic cloves and cook slowly, stirring often, until caramelized, 12 to 15 minutes. Add the wine, bring to a boil over high heat, and cook for 2 minutes. Add the reserved tomatoes, thyme, marjoram, and crushed red pepper. Stir in the clam juice and cook over high heat for 2 to 3 minutes.

5. Spread the vegetables evenly over the bottom of the pot and rest the pork loin on top of the vegetables. Transfer it to the oven and roast, basting every 10 to 15 minutes, until an instant-read thermometer inserted in the thickest part of the loin reads between 145°F and 150°F, about 45 minutes, for medium; or 160°F for more well done. Transfer the pork to a cutting board, cover with aluminum foil, and set aside.

6. Put the pot over medium heat. Add the clams, cover, and cook until the clams pop open, 5 to 6 minutes.

7. While the clams are cooking, carve the loin into individual chops and arrange decoratively on a platter. When the clams are done, arrange them over and around the chops.

8. To serve, spoon some sauce around the platter and scatter the chopped parsley over the pork and vegetables. Serve family style from the center of the table.

Braised Pork Loin with Artichokes

■ *Serves 4* ■

This is a variation on the classic French *barigoule* in which artichokes are braised in a white wine–olive oil broth. Once reduced, the braising liquid becomes an acidic sauce, the perfect match for the artichokes' flavor. Here, this technique is used to make a main course with the addition of pork loin. Don't be afraid to keep the pork a bit pink at the center; it's perfectly safe and will keep it from drying out.

One 4-pound boneless pork loin
3 cloves garlic, peeled and cut into
    thin slivers
Coarse salt
Freshly ground black pepper
½ cup olive oil
2 large Spanish onions, peeled and cut
    into 8 wedges each
1 (750 ml) bottle dry white wine
1 tablespoon chopped fresh thyme
    leaves
1 tablespoon chopped fresh oregano
    leaves

6 globe artichokes, outer leaves and
    choke removed, cut into quarters
    (see note, page 189)
1 quart store-bought, reduced-sodium
    chicken broth or homemade
    Chicken Stock (page 244)
2 tablespoons chopped fresh flat-leaf
    parsley leaves
2 lemons, peeled and cut crosswise
    into ½-inch slices

1. Preheat the oven to 400°F. Using a sharp, thin-bladed knife, make small, ½-inch-deep slits all over the pork loin. Slide a garlic sliver into each slit with the edge of the knife, using one-quarter of the slivered garlic for this purpose. Season the pork all over with salt and pepper.

2. Heat the olive oil in a large, heavy-bottomed ovenproof pot over medium-high heat. Add the pork loin and brown it on all sides, about 4 minutes per side. Remove the loin from the pot and set aside.

3. Drain off all but 2 tablespoons of fat from the pot. Add the onions and remaining garlic and cook over medium-high heat, stirring, for 4 minutes until softened. Add a splash of the white wine, stir to loosen up the ingredients, and scrape up any browned bits stuck to the bottom of the pot. Add the thyme and oregano. Continue to add the wine in small increments, stirring after each addition and adding more only after the previous addition has evaporated.

4. When nearly all of the wine has evaporated, return the loin to the pot and add the artichoke quarters. Pour in the broth and bring to a boil over high heat. Cover, transfer to the oven, and braise for 50 minutes to 1 hour, until the pork reaches an internal temperature of 145°F to 150°F on an instant-read thermometer inserted in its thickest section, for medium, or 160°F for more well done. Transfer the pork to a cutting board, cover with aluminum foil, and let rest for 5 minutes. If the artichokes are not done (a sharp, thin-bladed knife should pierce easily to their center), return the pot to the oven and cook for another few minutes.

5. To serve, slice the loin into 8 pieces. Place 2 pieces in each of 4 shallow bowls. Add a few artichoke quarters to each bowl. Stir the parsley into the sauce and spoon some sauce over each serving. Garnish with the lemon slices.

ARTICHOKES

To prepare artichokes, first fill a large bowl with cold water and squeeze the juice from half a lemon into it. Pull off the tough outer leaves of the artichoke and use a heavy knife to remove the stem, if any. Cut the choke just above the heart, about 1½ inches from the stem end. Use a paring knife to trim away the green leaves until you get down to the yellow part, which is where the heart begins. Cut the artichoke in half lengthwise, scoop out the hairy choke, then cut in quarters. Place the quarters in the lemon water to keep them from discoloring until ready to use.

Pork Medallions with Barbecue Sauce

■ Serves 4 ■

The sauce in this recipe is a riff on the one I helped develop for Bubba's, a barbecue joint owned by my Ouest-restaurant partners. It's more simple than the kind of sauce you'd encounter in the nation's bastions of barbecue, but a relatively quick way to make your own from scratch. If you don't want to fire up the grill, cook the medallions in a sauté pan over medium high heat for five to six minutes per side for medium-rare, seven to eight minutes for more well done.

2 pork tenderloins (about 1 pound each) halved crosswise	1½ cups tomato ketchup
3 cloves garlic, peeled and thinly sliced	¼ cup molasses
¼ cup olive oil	¼ cup chipotle chiles in adobo, pureed in a blender
1 quart water	4 teaspoons Worcestershire sauce
4 large Spanish onions, peeled and cut into small dice	¼ teaspoon Tabasco sauce
2 cups cider vinegar	½ teaspoon cumin seeds
¼ cup light brown sugar	Coarse salt
	Freshly ground black pepper

1. Put the pork medallions in a baking dish. Scatter the garlic slices over the pork and drizzle with the olive oil. Cover and let marinate in the refrigerator for 2 to 3 hours.

2. Bring the water to a boil in a large, heavy-bottomed pot over high heat. Add the onions and boil until tender, 2 to 3 minutes. Remove the onions with a slotted spoon and discard.

3. Gradually stir the vinegar and brown sugar into the boiling water and let boil for 5 minutes. Stir in the ketchup, molasses, chipotle puree, Worcestershire sauce, Tabasco sauce, and cumin seeds. Remove the pot from the heat. If not serving immediately, let cool, cover, and refrigerate for a few days or freeze for up to 1 month. Reheat before proceeding.

4. Remove the pork medallions from the refrigerator and let come to room temperature. Set aside half of the sauce. Prepare an outdoor grill for grilling.

5. Brush off the garlic slices and excess oil from the pork medallions, season them on both sides with salt and pepper, and place them on the grate over the hottest part of the grill. Grill, basting with the remaining half of the barbecue sauce, for about 5 minutes on each side.

6. To serve, place 1 pork portion on each of 4 plates and serve the reserved barbecue sauce alongside.

Braised Pork Belly in White Wine Sauce

■ Serves 6 ■

Pork belly is essentially bacon before it becomes bacon: It's the fatty, tasty portion of the pig before it's cured or smoked (see Mail-Order Sources, page 247). Given this fact, it's probably not surprising that a little of it goes a long way, so don't be alarmed that this recipe doesn't look like it makes enough for six people. Believe me, they'll all be satisfied, especially thanks to the extra dimensions of texture and flavor added by the easy step of coating the pork with mustard and bread crumbs.

Worth special mention here are the vegetables, which take on some of the pork's flavor during their time together in the oven, becoming meltingly tender and intensely rich and flavorful.

One 2-pound piece pork belly, tough outer skin removed

Coarse salt

Freshly ground black pepper

3 sprigs thyme, plus 1 teaspoon fresh thyme leaves

3 sprigs marjoram or oregano

10 cloves garlic, thinly sliced

3 tablespoons olive oil

3 stalks celery, peeled, cut on the bias into 1-inch pieces

1 large Spanish onion, peeled and cut into 6 wedges

1 large carrot, cut on the bias into 1-inch pieces

1 bay leaf

12 green peppercorns packed in brine, rinsed and drained, optional

2 cups dry white wine

3 tablespoons Dijon mustard

½ cup dried bread crumbs

1. Season the pork belly with salt and pepper and press the thyme sprigs, marjoram, and about 1 tablespoon of the sliced garlic into the flesh. Cover and let marinate in the refrigerator for 1 hour, or overnight.

2. Preheat the oven to 325°F.

3. Heat the olive oil in a heavy-bottomed pot just large enough to hold the pork belly until hot but not yet smoking. Scrape off and discard the herb sprigs and garlic from the pork and add the pork to the pan, skin side down. Cook for 5 minutes to render the fat (you don't want to brown the pork). Turn and cook on the other side for 5 minutes. Transfer the pork to a plate and set aside.

4. Pour off all but a few tablespoons of fat from the pan. Add the celery, onion, carrot, bay leaf, peppercorns, if using, remaining garlic, and the thyme leaves to the pot and cook over medium heat, stirring occasionally, until lightly browned, about 10 minutes. Add the wine and bring to a boil over high heat. Cook over medium-high heat for 5 to 6 minutes or until the liquid is reduced by half.

5. Return the pork to the pot, cover, and braise in the oven for 1 hour. Remove the cover and braise for another 45 minutes to 1 hour until the meat is very tender and the vegetables are soft. Transfer the pork to a cutting board and cover with aluminum foil to keep warm. If not serving immediately, let cool, cover, and refrigerate for a few days or freeze for up to 1 month. Reheat before proceeding.

6. Preheat the broiler. While the broiler is heating, pick out and discard the bay leaf from the pot. Transfer the vegetables to a bowl, using a slotted spoon to let any excess fat drain off. Cover the vegetables to keep them warm.

7. Slice the pork crosswise into 6 equal pieces. Lay each slice on its side on a rimmed baking sheet and smear with some mustard. Sprinkle with bread crumbs and broil until golden brown, 1 to 2 minutes.

8. To serve, place a 1 slice of meat on each of 6 warm plates and spoon some vegetables alongside.

VARIATION

Braised Pork Chops in White Wine Sauce

I beg you to try pork belly, but if it just doesn't appeal to you, you can make this recipe with pork chops: Use 4 double-cut pork chops instead of the pork belly. Season them well with salt and pepper and brown in ¼ cup hot olive oil in a sauté pan over medium-high heat. In a large pot, make the braising liquid, starting with Step 4 and heating 2 tablespoons olive oil in the pot before adding the vegetables. Add the seared pork chops to the liquid and cook for 15 to 18 minutes for medium doneness. Remove them from the pot and proceed with the mustard, bread crumbs, and browning.

Braised Veal with Tuna Sauce

■ Serves 4 ■

This is my take on the classic Italian *vitello tonnato,* or veal with tuna sauce. That dish might sound odd if you've never tried it, but the combination of succulent veal and creamy, salty tuna sauce are a match made in heaven. The original is actually a chilled, lasagna-like casserole with layers of thinly sliced braised veal alternating with tuna sauce, but many modern chefs present it more simply with the veal arranged carpaccio style on a plate and the sauce drizzled over it.

I look at veal and tuna sauce as a make-ahead item perfect year-round for buffets. Make it a day in advance then serve it at room temperature or grill it to reheat. Leaving a small quantity of fat on a lean meat like veal helps keep it moist as it cooks, so don't trim it too closely.

1 cup olive oil

2 pounds veal breast, trimmed of most
    excess fat

Coarse salt

Freshly ground black pepper

All-purpose flour, for dredging

15 cloves garlic, peeled, plus ½ clove,
    peeled and minced

2 anchovy fillets packed in oil, rinsed
    and patted dry, plus 4 fillets,
    minced

2 bay leaves

1 tablespoon black peppercorns

3 sprigs thyme

2½ cups dry white wine

1 scant tablespoon distilled white
    vinegar (page 246)

2 tablespoons capers, plus more
    for garnish, drained but not
    rinsed

Two 5½-ounce cans Italian tuna
    packed in oil

1 cup mayonnaise

1. Preheat the oven to 325°F. Season the veal breast all over with salt and pepper. Dredge it in flour, shaking off any excess.

2. Heat the olive oil over medium-high heat in a heavy-bottomed pot large enough to hold the veal breast comfortably. Add the veal breast to the pot and slowly brown it on all sides, 3 to 4 minutes per side, taking care not to scorch or burn the flour. Remove the veal and set aside.

3. Drain all but 2 tablespoons of fat from the pan. Stir in the whole garlic cloves, whole anchovy fillets, bay leaves, peppercorns, and thyme. Stir in the wine, vinegar, and 1½ tablespoons salt, raise the heat to high, and cook until the wine begins to boil.

4. Return the veal to the pot. As soon as the wine returns to a simmer, cover the pot and transfer it to the oven. Braise until the veal is fork-tender, 2 to 2½ hours. Check the pot periodically to be sure the liquid is simmering very gently; if it's bubbling rapidly, lower the oven temperature to 300°F.

5. While the veal is in the oven, make the tuna sauce: Combine the tuna, capers, minced anchovies, and minced garlic in a blender and process until smooth. Pour the mayonnaise into a bowl and stir in the tuna mixture. If the sauce seems too thick—it should have the consistency of heavy cream—stir in a tablespoon or 2 of warm tap water to thin it until pourable. Cover and refrigerate until chilled, about 1 hour, or for up to 24 hours.

6. Transfer the veal to a cutting board and let it cool to room temperature. Discard the braising liquid. If not serving immediately, let cool, cover, and refrigerate the veal and sauce separately for up to 24 hours.

7. To serve, slice the veal breast into ½-inch-thick slices, divide the slices among 4 plates, and spoon a thin layer of tuna sauce over each serving.

VARIATION

For an easy but starkly different variation, grill the veal slices over high heat for 1 minute on each side before serving.

Herb-Stuffed Veal Breast

■ *Serves 6* ■

I love this technique for cooking veal breast, because it hits the meat with herbaceous flavor from within and from the outside. The boneless breast is spread with thyme, garlic, and cheese, which infuse the meat with flavor as it braises in a mixture of vegetables, vinegar, wine, and stock. Because it looks so impressive when sliced, this is one of those one-pot dishes that can be served at the most elegant of dinner parties.

4 plum tomatoes, quartered lengthwise
Coarse salt
Freshly ground black pepper
Sugar
2 small boneless breasts of veal (about 2½ pounds each)
4 cloves garlic, peeled and thinly sliced, plus 10 cloves, smashed and peeled
2 tablespoons freshly grated Parmesan cheese
Pinch plus 1 teaspoon fresh thyme leaves

1 cup olive oil
1 large Spanish onion, peeled and cut into 6 wedges
2 large carrots, peeled and cut on the bias into 1-inch pieces
1 bottle (750 ml) dry white wine
1 tablespoon distilled white vinegar (page 246)
2 bay leaves
¼ cup fresh flat-leaf parsley leaves
1 cup store-bought, reduced-sodium chicken broth, beef broth, or homemade Chicken Stock (page 244)

1. About 30 minutes before you want to cook, put the tomatoes in a bowl and season with salt, pepper, and sugar. Season the inside of the veal breast with salt, pepper, the sliced garlic cloves, the grated Parmesan, and a pinch of thyme leaves. Set the tomatoes and veal aside at room temperature.

2. Preheat the oven to 325°F.

3. Roll the veal breast up lengthwise and tie it at 2-inch intervals with kitchen string. Season the outside with salt and pepper.

4. Heat the olive oil in a large, heavy-bottomed ovenproof pot over medium-high heat. Add the veal and brown on all sides, 3 to 4 minutes per side. Remove the veal and set aside.

5. Drain all but 2 tablespoons of fat from the pot. Add the onion, carrots, and smashed garlic cloves and cook, stirring, over medium heat until lightly browned, 8 to 10 minutes.

6. Add the wine and vinegar and stir to scrape up any browned bits stuck to the bottom of the pot. Add the tomatoes, bay leaves and parsley. Stir in the broth, 1 tablespoon salt, and 1 teaspoon pepper. Bring to a boil, then return the veal to the pot. When the liquid returns to the boil, cover the pot, and transfer to the oven. Braise for about 90 minutes, until an instant-read thermometer inserted into the thickest part of the breast reads 160°F.

7. Transfer the veal to a cutting board, snip off the strings, cover with aluminum foil to keep warm, and let rest while you finish the sauce.

8. Discard the bay leaf from the sauce. Let the sauce settle, then skim off any fat that rises to the surface.

9. To serve, slice the veal into ½-inch-thick slices and divide them among 4 warm dinner plates. Carefully remove the vegetables from the pot and arrange them around the veal. Spoon some sauce over and around the meat and vegetables and serve at once.

VARIATION

Mushroom and Spinach-Stuffed Veal Beast

Replace the Parmesan cheese and garlic with the mushroom and spinach filling from Andrew and Caitlin's Soppressata Lasagna (page 127, Step 4).

Veal Shank Braised in
White Sauce with Mushrooms

■ *Serves 4* ■

A blanquette is a white stew in which none of the ingredients, including the meat, are browned. It can be made with any number of meats, but is most famously prepared with veal. While I enjoy the flavor of a blanquette, I find the small cubes with which it's made just don't satisfy me. I'm also powerless to resist the temptation to brown any cut of meat once I get it into the pot. But I do love that white stew . . .

So, this recipe applies the flavors and textures of a *blanquette de veau* to osso buco, or center-cut veal shanks, the heartiest cut of veal known to man and the one used in the braised dish of the same name. The result is dramatically different from the traditional *blanquette de veau,* with a powerful contrast between the seared hunk of meat and the light, white sauce, which I've enriched here with the addition of porcini mushrooms and crème fraîche.

If you don't have a cooking vessel large enough to hold four shanks, you can divide the ingredients between two smaller pots.

4 center-cut veal shanks (12 to 16 ounces each), tied firmly around the equator with kitchen string to keep them from falling apart when cooked (they may be sold this way)
Coarse salt
Freshly ground black pepper
All-purpose flour, for dredging
¾ cup olive oil
2 stalks celery, cut into small dice
1 large Spanish onion, peeled and cut into small dice
1 large leek, white part plus 1 inch green, cut into 1-inch pieces, washed well, and dried

½ large carrot, peeled and cut into small dice
8 cloves garlic, smashed and peeled
1 tablespoon green peppercorns packed in brine, rinsed and drained
2 bay leaves
1 cup dry white wine
⅔ cup dried porcini mushrooms (page 243), rinsed, or dried black trumpet mushrooms
1 quart store-bought, reduced-sodium chicken broth or homemade Chicken Stock (page 244)
1 cup crème fraîche
2 tablespoons minced fresh chives

1. Preheat the oven to 350°F. Season the veal shanks liberally on all sides with salt and pepper. Dredge the veal shanks in flour to coat them all over, pressing down a bit to ensure that the flour adheres to the meat. Shake off any excess flour.

2. Heat the olive oil in a large ovenproof pot over medium-high heat until hot but not smoking. Add the veal shanks to the pot and brown well on all sides, 3 to 4 minutes per side. (Kitchen tongs are ideal for turning the shanks.) Transfer the shanks to a plate and set aside.

3. Add the celery, onion, leek, carrot, garlic, peppercorns, and bay leaves to the pot. Cook, stirring often and scraping up any browned bits stuck to the bottom of the pot, until the vegetables are softened but not browned, about 7 minutes.

4. Add the wine, bring to a boil over high heat, and cook, stirring, until nearly completely evaporated, 3 to 4 minutes. Stir in the porcini. Add the chicken broth and bring to a boil, skimming any scum that rises to the surface.

5. Return the shanks to the pot and transfer the pot to the oven. Braise until the shanks are fork-tender, 2 to 2½ hours. Every half hour, give the shanks a half-turn and check to be sure the liquid is simmering very gently; if it is bubbling rapidly, lower the oven temperature to 325°F.

6. Transfer the shanks to a cutting board; snip off and discard the kitchen string. Cover them with aluminum foil to keep warm while you prepare the sauce.

7. Strain the sauce through a colander set over a large bowl. Discard the vegetables. You should have approximately 1 cup of slightly thickened, richly flavored sauce. If you have any more, return it to the pot, bring to a boil over high heat, and reduce to thicken further and concentrate the flavors. Season with salt and pepper. If not serving immediately, let the sauce cool, cover it, and refrigerate it for up to 2 days. Wrap each shank in plastic wrap and refrigerate them as well. Reheat the meat on a rimmed baking sheet under the broiler and the sauce over low heat on the stovetop before proceeding.

8. Whisk the crème fraîche and chives into the sauce.

9. To serve, place 1 veal shank in the center of each of 4 dinner plates and spoon some sauce over and around the shanks.

VARIATION

Small white mushrooms and pearl onions are the classic garnish for *blanquette de veau*. If you like, throw some of those into the cooking liquid during the last hour of cooking. You can also sprinkle chopped, fresh herbs such as parsley and thyme over the finished dish.

Veal Kidneys with Red Wine and Shallot

■ *Serves 4* ■

I'll be honest. I wasn't exactly in love with veal kidney when I first tasted it. But you know what? I wasn't over the moon for caviar the first time I tasted it, either. Today, I love them both. So, if you like caviar, listen up while I try to sell you on one of my favorite indulgences.

The dense texture of veal kidney is unlike anything else I've ever eaten. I'm convinced that anyone who doesn't like veal kidney has simply never had one properly cooked, which is to say gently cooked with a little blush remaining at the middle. (Most people cook them to death.) The strong flavor of these kidneys calls for a powerful sauce, like this one fashioned from red wine and mustard.

When shopping for veal kidneys, look for shiny, plump, deep red candidates, passing by any slightly browned or shriveled ones. You can also, and will probably have to, order these by mail (see Mail-Order Sources, page 247).

2 tablespoons olive oil
2 veal kidneys (12 ounces each)
Coarse salt
Freshly ground black pepper
2 tablespoons unsalted butter
2 large shallots, peeled and minced
¼ cups light, sharp red wine, such as
   Chianti

1 teaspoon sugar
1 cup store-bought, reduced-sodium
   beef broth
1 tablespoon whole-grain mustard
1 tablespoon chopped fresh flat-leaf
   parsley leaves

1. Preheat the oven to 275°F.

2. In a wide, shallow sauté pan (which will allow the sauce to reduce as quickly as possible later on), warm the olive oil over medium-high heat. Season the kidneys with salt and pepper. Add the kidneys to the pan and brown them very well on one side, 4 to 5 minutes. Add 1 tablespoon of the butter to the skillet, flip the kidneys, and brown on the other side, about 4 minutes.

3. Transfer the kidneys to a rimmed baking sheet and place in the oven, leaving the door slightly ajar. You just want to keep them warm while you prepare the sauce.

4. Lower the heat under the sauté pan to medium and add the shallots. Cook until softened and translucent, 3 to 5 minutes. Add the red wine and sugar and stir to loosen any browned bits stuck to the bottom of the pan. Bring to a boil over high heat, and cook until reduced almost to a glaze.

5. Add the broth, bring to a boil, and cook until reduced by half. Whisk in the mustard, and then stir in the remaining 1 tablespoon butter. Season with salt and pepper, remove from the heat, and cover to keep warm.

6. To serve, slice and fan out half a kidney on each of 4 warm dinner plates and spoon some sauce over and around the slices. Sprinkle the parsley on top.

Accompaniments
and **Additions**

This section highlights some of my favorite ways to embellish a dish or meal with accompaniments that can be served alongside fish and meats, and additions that can be stirred right into soups and stews or used to creatively expand all sorts of leftovers.

I'm such a believer in applying accompaniments to more than one recipe, that I offer them à la carte on my menu at Ouest for customers who want to choose another dish to round out their meal. Accompaniments are fun. When served family style, they enhance the communal experience of dining as the platter or bowl is passed from person to person and everyone helps him- or herself to a portion. A well-chosen accompaniment takes the meal to a whole new level; for example, I love starchy accompaniments including Mashed Potatoes (page 221) and Polenta (page 210) that soak up any extra sauce on the plate.

I separate out accompaniments in my restaurants and in this book because they're not absolutely essential, but they are appealing. My taste here runs to the traditional, but I make all of my accompaniments in my own style; the cream for my Potato Gratin (page 222), for example, is infused with black pepper and thyme so the gratin's flavor is unusually complex. In other words, even though their names might be familiar, the recipes that follow are a bit different from others you might have seen.

When I talk about additions, I usually mean grains and pasta, which I add to most of the soups and stews I cook at home, either to bring another texture or flavor to the bowl, or to expand leftovers into another main course. I also like turning leftover braised meats into something new by making them the basis for a pasta dish. In the pages that follow, you'll learn how to do this as well. Also included in this section are some helpful tips for precooking grains and pastas so you can have them ready to be reheated in whatever dish you'll be adding them to, rather than waiting for them to cook from a raw state.

Finally, I should explain that accompaniments and additions aren't absolute categories. Obviously, most grains and pastas can be served as accompaniments, and while the converse isn't always true, it can sometimes spark great innovations, like using Mashed Potatoes (page 221) as an addition to Potato and Leek Soup (page 44). I don't find these overlaps confusing; in fact, I adore them because they remind me how infinitely flexible home cooking can be.

Grains

Technically speaking, grains are the fruits of grasses, which we adopt in many ways for cooking. Whole grains (also called kernels, berries, or groats) have the bran and germ intact, while coarsely ground kernels are referred to as meal. Barley is a grain, as is cornmeal. There are also a number of foods which are not, strictly speaking, grains, but which are considered grains in the culinary world, including millet (a seed) and couscous, which is actually tiny bits of semolina pasta.

Given this variety, it's important to note that some grains are more appropriate as additions; others more suitable as accompaniments. The following list includes my favorite grains and methods for cooking them.

Barley

■ Makes 1 cup, enough to add to 2 quarts of soup ■

Barley, a nutty-flavored, off-white grain, is a special addition to soup. I prefer pearl barley—with the hull and bran removed. It can almost always be cooked in the soup itself: Add ½ cup barley per 2 quarts of soup during the final 45 minutes of cooking. This saves you the step of precooking the barley on its own and imbues the barley with the flavor of the soup itself.

If you want to precook barley to add it to hot leftover soup or stew, follow this recipe:

½ **cup pearl barley**
2½ **cups water**
Coarse salt

1. Put the barley in a pot and add the water and a pinch or 2 of salt. Bring to a boil over high heat, then lower the heat, cover, and simmer until the barley is softened but still a bit al dente, about 45 minutes.

2. Drain or, if not serving immediately, cool under cold running water, drain, and keep at room temperature for up to 2 hours or cover and refrigerate overnight. Let come to room temperature before using.

Add to: Mushroom, Barley, and Sage Soup (page 32), Turkey Soup with Stuffing Dumplings (page 64).

Couscous

Makes about 4 cups couscous,
■ enough to serve 4 as a side dish (see Note) ■

Couscous is referred to as a grain but in reality it's pellet-size pasta that originated in North Africa. I use it as an addition to soups and stews and also an accompaniment to dishes with a Mediterranean or Moroccan influence. If I'm serving a brothy dish, I use some of the simmering cooking liquid to cook the couscous, as in Cod with Tomato, Saffron Broth, Leeks, and Couscous (page 148). This method is great for flavoring and preparing couscous that will be served alongside poached, stewed, or braised fish and meats.

2 cups water
One 10-ounce package, quick-cooking
    couscous (about 1½ cups)
Coarse salt

1. Bring the water to a boil in a pot over high heat. Put the couscous in a bowl. Pour just enough of the boiling water into the bowl to come up to the top of the couscous. Season with a pinch of salt, stir once, and cover with plastic wrap. Let steam until the liquid is absorbed, about 5 minutes.
2. Remove the plastic and fluff the couscous with a fork. If not using immediately, keep at room temperature for up to 2 hours or let cool, cover, and refrigerate overnight. Let come to room temperature before using.

Serve with: Roasted Fish and Shellfish with Tomatoes and Parsley (page 98), Baked Sea Bass, Papillote Style, with Lemon and Olives (page 146), Moroccan-Spice-Braised Lamb Shanks (page 167).

Note: Use 1½ packages (2¼ cups) couscous and 3 cups water to serve 6 as an accompaniment. For enough to add to 2 quarts of soup or stew, use ½ cup couscous and 1 cup water.

Israeli couscous

Israeli couscous is a larger couscous that is more durable and toothsome than "regular" couscous, so it is more suitable as an accompaniment than an addition. To make about 4 cups of Israeli couscous, enough to serve 4 as a side dish, bring 2 cups of water to a boil in a small pot over high heat. Add a pinch of salt and 1⅓ cups Israeli couscous and cook, stirring, until tender but still a bit al dente, 6 to 8 minutes. Drain or, if not serving immediately, cool under cold running water, drain, and set aside at room temperature for up to 2 hours, or cover and refrigerate overnight. It is especially delicious as an accompaniment to Simmered Shrimp Sauté with Shiitake Mushrooms and Scallions (page 141).

Millet

Makes about 1¼ cups millet, or
▪ enough to add to 2 quarts of soup or stew (see Note) ▪

Popular in Africa and Asia, millet is a good alternative to rice or couscous. Like barley, you can cook it directly in a soup or stew—it takes about 30 minutes to become nicely al dente—and can also cook it on its own for adding to leftover soups and stews.

1½ cups water
½ cup millet
Coarse salt

1. Pour the water into a small pot and bring to a boil over high heat. Stir in the millet, season with a pinch or 2 of salt, and cover. Lower the heat and simmer until the water has been absorbed by the millet, about 30 minutes.

2. Drain or, if not serving immediately, cool under cold running water, drain, and set aside at room temperature for up to 2 hours, or cover and refrigerate overnight. Let come to room temperature before using.

Add to: Roasted Fish and Shellfish with Tomatoes and Parsley (page 98), Beer and Beef Stew (page 116).

Serve with: Baked Sea Bass, Papillote Style, with Lemon and Olives (page 146), Moroccan-Spice-Braised Lamb Shanks (page 167).

Note: Triple this recipe for enough millet to serve 4 as an accompaniment; quadruple it to serve 6.

Polenta

■ Serves 4 as a side dish ■

Polenta, sometimes referred to as "Italian grits," is cooked cornmeal. This is my basic recipe for polenta, which can be made with yellow cornmeal or the more unusual (and sometimes harder to find) white cornmeal, which has a less-pronounced flavor. This recipe produces a rather loose polenta that I like because it practically becomes one with any sauce it's served with. For a firmer polenta, double the amount of cornmeal. You can also produce a less creamy version by using chicken or vegetable broth instead of milk.

2½ cups whole milk
1 tablespoon unsalted butter
1 clove garlic, peeled and minced
2 teaspoons coarse salt
1 teaspoon freshly ground black pepper
½ cup cornmeal, yellow or white

1. Pour the milk into a pot over high heat and add the butter, garlic, salt, and pepper. Bring to a boil, then reduce the heat until the liquid is just simmering. Whisk in the cornmeal gradually and continue to cook, whisking until the polenta is thick, 12 to 15 minutes.

2. Serve at once, or keep warm in a covered double boiler set over simmering water for up to 2 hours.

Serve with: Baked Chicken with Bacon, Mushrooms, and Pearl Onions (page 150), Florentine Pot Roast with Red Wine, Mushrooms, and Tomatoes (page 178).

Rice

A lot of us are used to seeing rice—yes, it's a grain as well—served as a side dish, especially those of us who order Chinese food on a regular basis. I don't find rice terribly interesting on its own, but I treasure it as an addition to soups and stews where it brings a little extra texture to every mouthful.

Brown Rice

Makes about 1½ cups,
■ enough to add to 2 quarts of soup or stew (see Note) ■

Brown rice, which is actually the same grain as white rice but with the bran and germ intact, has an understated earthy flavor and an appealing, slightly chewy texture. It's delicious in chili and added to brothy soups.

1½ **cups water**
1 **cup brown rice**
Coarse salt

1. Put the water in a heavy-bottomed pot and bring to a boil over high heat. Add the rice and a pinch or 2 of salt, stir once, lower the heat, cover, and cook at a slow simmer until the liquid has been absorbed and the rice is fluffy, 15 to 20 minutes.

2. Fluff the rice with a fork. If not using immediately, keep at room temperature for up to 2 hours or let cool, cover, and refrigerate overnight. Let come to room temperature before using.

Add to: Lemon and Egg Drop Soup (page 42), Turkey Soup with Stuffing Dumplings (in place of the dumplings, page 64), Texas-Style Chili (page 114), Venison Chili (page 128).

Note: Triple this recipe for enough rice to serve 4 as an accompaniment; quadruple it to serve 6.

Long-Grain White Rice

Makes about 1½ cups,
■ enough to add to 2 quarts of soup or stew (see Note) ■

The kernels of long-grain rice remain distinct when cooked, unlike those of medium-grain rice including arborio (used to make risotto) or short-grain sushi rice, where the starch binds the kernels together. This quality makes it a perfect add-in to brothy soups.

1½ cups water
½ cup long-grain rice
Coarse salt

1. Put the water in a heavy-bottomed pot and bring to a boil over high heat. Add the rice and a pinch or 2 of salt, stir once, lower the heat, cover, and cook at a slow simmer until the liquid has been absorbed and the rice is fluffy, 15 to 20 minutes.

2. Fluff the rice with a fork. If not using immediately, keep at room temperature for up to 2 hours or let cool, cover, and refrigerate overnight. Let come to room temperature before using.

Add to: Lemon and Egg Drop Soup (page 42), Lobster Bisque (page 57).

Note: Triple this recipe for enough rice to serve 4 as an accompaniment; quadruple it to serve 6.

Wild Rice

Makes about 4 cups,
■ enough to serve 4 as a side dish (see Note) ■

A type of grass, wild rice is a great addition to brothy soups when you want to add a firmer texture and more pronounced flavor than either white or brown rice can offer.

Wild rice is also the one rice I love as an accompaniment: Its nutty flavor and firm bite is the perfect match for game and game birds. For this reason, I'm offering a recipe that makes enough to serve as a side dish.

1½ **cups wild rice**
About 4 cups store-bought, reduced-sodium
    vegetable or chicken broth or homemade
    Vegetable or Chicken Stock (page 244)
Coarse salt
Freshly ground black pepper

1. Put the rice in a heavy-bottomed pot, add the broth, and bring the liquid to a boil over high heat. Lower the heat, cover, and cook at a slow simmer until the rice plumps and fluffs up and the kernels are cracked, 30 to 50 minutes. You might have to add extra broth or some water during this time if the liquid is absorbed before the rice is done.

2. Fluff the rice with a fork, and season with salt and pepper. If not using immediately, keep at room temperature for up to 2 hours or let cool, cover, and refrigerate overnight. Let come to room temperature before using.

Serve with: Duck with Dried Fruits (page 162).

Add to: Turkey Soup with Stuffing Dumplings (page 64).

Note: Halve this recipe for enough rice to add to 2 quarts of soup or stew; for enough to serve 6 as a side dish, use 3 cups rice and about 6½ cups broth.

Pasta

For most people, pasta is woefully one-dimensional: A bowl of noodles tossed with some kind of tomato sauce. Me, I could write an epic poem about my love for the endless variety of pasta dishes out there. (It wouldn't be very good, but I *could* write it.) But for our purposes, I'll confine myself to pasta's value in relation to the recipes in this book.

When it comes to pasta, there are good things to be said for both dried and fresh. The difference between the two isn't nearly as great as that between fresh and dried herbs. Tell a serious foodie that you use dried herbs and he or she'll give you a cautionary lecture that'll send shivers down your spine, linking dried herbs to the decline of civilization, or at the very least admonishing you for using flavorless dust that's been sitting in your cupboard since Carter was president. Not so, dried pasta. In fact, in many ways, dried has more to offer than fresh (see "Dried Pasta" and "Fresh Pasta," below).

As for cooking fresh or dried pasta, the method's the same for both.

▪ Makes enough to serve 6 as a side dish, or 4 as a main course ▪

6 quarts water
2 tablespoons coarse salt
1 pound pasta

1. Bring the water to a rolling boil. Add the salt, and then add the pasta. Cover the pot and let the water return to a boil, then uncover and cook until the pasta is tender, following the directions on the package, or shaving 1 minute off the cooking time for dried pasta to ensure the pasta remains pleasingly chewy, or al dente. (If using homemade fresh pasta or fresh pasta with no instructions on the package, it will take 2 to 4 minutes to cook, test for doneness by removing a piece with tongs or a slotted spoon, cooling it under cold running water, and taking a bite.)

2. Drain and serve or toss with hot sauces. Or, if not serving immediately, rinse under cold, running water to wash away the starch and prevent the pasta from clinging to itself, and set aside for up to 2 hours at room temperature. Cooked, dried pasta

can be refrigerated overnight in an airtight container, but do not store cooked, fresh pasta overnight or it will become unpleasantly glutinous.

Dried Pasta

For my money, the greatest attribute of dried pasta is that it's the one capable of truly reaching that paradise stage of doneness called al dente, which means "to the tooth," or just pleasantly chewy. Thanks to this fact alone, as far as I'm concerned, dried pasta has bragging rights over fresh.

Dried pasta is also exceedingly user-friendly, almost to the point of obsequiousness. If you're planning to add pasta to one of the recipes in this book, you should precook it rather than cooking it right in the pot to keep the starch from clouding the liquid. (See instructions, page 218.) When you're ready to use it, just add it to the dish at hand, where it'll warm through in a matter of seconds.

As for which pasta to add to which dishes, it all depends on how much you want the pasta to stand out. If you want to turn a stew or leftover braised or roasted meat into a "Pasta and . . ." affair, then opt for a larger or longer pasta like spaghetti (page 218) or fresh pastas like fettuccine, linguine, or pappardelle (page 219). When you simply want to add some texture to a soup or stew, look to the smaller pasta shapes such as pastina and orzo.

Capellini (Angel Hair)

Angel hair, the thinnest pasta, is shaped in long, wispy strands. Though angel hair provides less of a bite than I usually prefer, its delicate nature does tend to work well with shellfish sauces.

Serve with: Tuscan-Style Seafood Stew, as a Variation (page 60)

Ditalini, Orzo, Pastina (Acini di Pepe), Pennette, Tubetti, Tubettini

These small pastas are most often used in soups and I also enjoy adding them to stews. They are another exception to the throw-it-right-in approach described in the introduction, with the exception of pastina, which doesn't give off enough starch or increase enough in volume to be a problem.

I usually recommend precooking these pastas in 2 quarts of boiling water seasoned with 2 tablespoons coarse salt until al dente, then draining them and refreshing them under cold running water. This stops the cooking process and allows you to control how much volume they will add to the soup.

These varieties are largely interchangeable, but it's worth noting that pastina is the smallest, and orzo isn't much bigger. These two add a subtle, almost rice-like addition as opposed to the tubular, unmistakably pasta presence of the others.

Add to: Pasta and Bean Soup (page 24); Spinach, Parmesan, and Garlic Soup (page 34); Twice-Cooked Vegetable Soup (page 46); Roasted Fish and Shellfish with Tomatoes and Parsley (page 98, smaller pastina only); Rabbit Stew with Marjoram and Vermouth (page 130); Chicken in Hunter-Style Sauce (page 152); Mushroom-Poached Squab (page 164).

Egg Noodles

These are short, broad noodles that are thinner than most other pastas. They cook very quickly, in just 1 or 2 minutes, and are best used in their traditional role as a complement to bistro staples, especially those with a red wine sauce.

Serve with: Mushroom Stew (page 80), Beer and Beef Stew (page 116), Beef Stroganoff (page 122), Chicken in Red Wine Sauce (page 156).

Spaghetti

A bit wider than capellini (page 216), spaghetti is another of the most well-known pastas in America. In fact, it's probably the most familiar. I think it's so popular because of its average shape and size. Pappardelle (page 219) may be too wide for some people, capellini too narrow for others, but spaghetti is always a safe bet, making it the most versatile pasta. Ideal for tomato sauces, it's also a good—though in most cases not the best—choice for sauces based on everything from seafood to braised meats.

Serve with: Sautéed Calamari with White Wine, Garlic, and Clam Broth (page 100), Chicken Hearts and Gizzards in Italian-Style Tomato Sauce (page 104).

Fresh Pasta

Fresh pasta usually involves long, flat noodles, such as linguine, fettuccine, and pappardelle; filled pastas such as tortellini and ravioli; and shapes including my nominee for Best Name Ever, *strozzapreti,* which translates to "strangled priest." (Gee, I wonder what Sunday school was like for the chef who created that one.)

I usually use fresh pasta as an accompaniment, rather than stirring it into a dish. When it comes to leftovers, however, fresh pasta can turn yesterday's dinner into tonight's main course by stretching a surplus of stew, sauce, or meat into another meal. This is usually done by removing the poultry or meat from its sauce, roughly chopping it into bite-size pieces, returning it to the sauce, reheating, and tossing with freshly cooked hot pasta.

What follows are the fresh pastas referred to in this book, and examples of when I'd be most likely to call on them in the kitchen.

Fettuccine and Linguine

These are probably the most familiar fresh pasta shapes. They are both essentially long strands, although linguine is a bit narrower than fettuccine. I like these thin, flat noodles with relatively soupy sauces featuring gently flavored ingredients, like those with seafood and vegetables or those based on wine, broth, or tomatoes, as opposed to heavier cream sauces or sauces with braised meats.

Serve with: Sautéed Calamari with White Wine, Garlic, and Clam Broth (page 100), Simmered Shrimp Sauté with Shiitake Mushrooms and Scallions (page 141).

Pappardelle

This is probably the widest pasta that isn't reserved for lasagna or making ravioli. Pappardelle is usually served with rabbit stew or tossed with chopped, leftover braised meats and their braising liquid. Toss freshly cooked, hot pasta with the reheated liquid just before serving.

Add to: Florentine Pot Roast with Red Wine, Mushrooms, and Tomatoes (page 178), Braised Oxtail with Cipolline Onions (page 180), Braised Beef Cheeks (page 182).

Note: You might also think about substituting pappardelle for egg noodles. For example, dishes such as Chicken in Red Wine Sauce (page 156) and Rabbit Stew with Marjoram and Vermouth (page 130) pair exceedingly well with pappardelle, which soaks up the sauce the same way egg noodles do.

Ravioli

Ravioli are another great vehicle for using leftovers. If you make your own pasta dough, great. If not, it's no secret that you can purchase wonton skins from the refrigerated section of your market and use them for ravioli. You can also purchase freshly made pasta sheets from many gourmet stores and Italian markets. Use a sharp knife or pizza cutter to cut them into 3- or 4-inch squares. You can also make different shapes by cutting round ravioli using a 3- or 4-inch glass or biscuit-cutter, or by folding wonton skins diagonally into half-moon shaped dumplings called agnolotti.

To make ravioli, simply lay a square of pasta on a flat surface in front of you and brush the edges with egg yolk whisked together with 1 or 2 tablespoons of water. Put teaspoon-size portions of cooled filling in the center of the pasta square, top with another pasta square, and press the edges together by hand or seal them with a fork, leaving a small gap open. Gently squeeze each raviolo between the palms of your hands to expel any trapped air, then seal the gap closed.

Fresh ravioli can be refrigerated for up to 3 days, covered with plastic wrap. You can also freeze them for several months: Lay them in a single layer on a baking sheet that's been dusted with cornmeal and place in the freezer. When the ravioli are hard, after a few hours, transfer them to a bag, seal it, and keep in the freezer. When ready to cook, bring 2 quarts water to a gentle boil in a large pot, add 2 tablespoons salt and the ravioli, and cook until they rise to the surface. Use a slotted spoon to remove them from the water without breaking them.

Ideal for leftovers from: Braised Beef Cheeks (page 182), Florentine Pot Roast with Red Wine, Mushrooms, and Tomatoes (page 178).

Potatoes

Sliced, mashed, boiled, baked, or fried, I love potatoes. I think of them as the universal donor of accompaniments because there's almost no fish or meat dish that doesn't pair well with some form of cooked potato.

The following two potato side dishes are the most appropriate for the recipes in this book:

Mashed Potatoes

■ Serves 6 as a side dish ■

My recipe for mashed potatoes depends on hot milk and cold butter to create a richly textured potato puree that, perhaps surprisingly, isn't too heavy. The most important aspect of this recipe, as with all mashed potato recipes, is to season carefully with salt just until you taste a pronounced potato flavor but before the mixture tastes too salty. Feel free to vary the amounts of milk and butter to your liking, adding more milk for a looser puree, or more butter for a richer, thicker one.

> 3 pounds baking potatoes, peeled and cut
> into 1-inch dice
> Coarse salt
> 1½ cups whole milk
> 12 tablespoons (1½ sticks) unsalted butter,
> chilled and cut into very small dice
> Freshly ground black pepper

1. Preheat the oven to 250°F.

2. Put the diced potato in a large, heavy-bottomed pot and add enough water to cover by an inch or so. Season with salt and bring the water to a boil over high heat.

Lower the heat and simmer until the potatoes are tender when pierced with the tip of a sharp knife, but they still hold their shape, about 12 minutes.

3. Drain the potatoes in a colander and transfer them to a baking sheet. Bake in the oven until completely dried out, about 8 minutes. (This will intensify the potato flavor and keep the puree from being watery.)

4. While the potatoes are in the oven, heat the milk in a pot over medium-high heat; do not let it boil.

5. Remove the potatoes from the oven and pass them through a ricer into a bowl or put them in a bowl and mash them with a masher. Add a ladleful of the hot milk and about one-third of the butter. Mix the potatoes gently with a rubber spatula just until the butter and milk have been incorporated. Continue to add the remaining milk and butter in the same fashion.

6. Season with salt and pepper and serve immediately, or cover and keep warm for up to 2 hours in a double boiler set over simmering water.

Serve with: Potato and Leek Soup (page 44), Baked Chicken with Bacon, Mushrooms, and Pearl Onions (page 150), Mushroom-Braised Short Ribs (page 174), Braised Oxtail with Cipolline Onions (page 180), Braised Pork Shank (page 184).

Potato Gratin

■ Serves 6 as a side dish ■

This rich potato side dish, infused with black pepper and thyme, pairs exceptionally well with braised and roasted poultry and meats. It can be made a day or two in advance, and reheats well for great leftovers.

1 pint heavy cream or whole milk
12 garlic cloves, smashed and peeled
1 tablespoon black peppercorns
3 sprigs thyme

1 bay leaf
Coarse salt
Unsalted butter, for greasing dish
5 medium baking potatoes, peeled and cut
    crosswise into ⅛-inch-thick slices
Freshly ground black pepper

1. Pour the cream into a small pot and add the garlic, peppercorns, thyme, and bay leaf. Season with salt and bring to a simmer over low heat; do not let it boil. Simmer for 20 minutes to infuse the cream with flavor. Strain the cream and set it aside.

2. Preheat the oven to 375°F.

3. Butter a 12-inch round baking dish with sides at least 2 inches high. Arrange a layer of potato slices, overlapping slightly, on the bottom. Season with salt and pepper and spoon some seasoned cream over the top. Repeat with the remaining potatoes, seasoning each layer with salt and pepper and adding cream until the gratin is about 2 inches high, making sure to use all the cream. Press down gently on the potatoes to force some cream up over the top. If not baking immediately, cover and refrigerate for up to 2 days. Return to room temperature before proceeding.

4. Cover the dish with aluminum foil and bake in the oven for 40 minutes, or until a sharp, thin-bladed knife can easily pierce the center of the potatoes. Remove the foil and continue to bake just until the top is browned, 5 to 10 minutes.

5. Remove the gratin from the oven, slice into individual portions, and serve hot.

Serve with: Chicken in Red Wine Sauce (page 156), Beef Bourguignon (page 120), Mushroom-Braised Short Ribs (page 174), Seven-Hour Leg of Lamb (page 170).

Condiments
and Garnishes

Condiments and garnishes are a way to round out a dish at the last second, with a colorful, herbaceous drizzle; a crunchy, salty scattering; or another complementary flourish.

I don't add ingredients to a dish for the sake of their appearance alone, but there are certain flavor-packed condiments I also appreciate for their visual panache. In this section, you'll learn how to accent a variety of dishes with forest green Pesto (page 228), speckled with Parmesan cheese and pulverized pine nuts; creamy, glossy and garlicky Aïoli (page 230); rust-colored Saffron Aïoli (page 231); and neon Basil Oil (page 229). I also like condiments for their convenience; most of them can be made in advance and kept in the refrigerator for a last-second grab.

Unlike condiments, which can be stirred into a soup or stew, garnishes maintain their own identity as a dish is consumed. A sucker for textural and temperature contrasts, I'm partial to crunchy garnishes. Fried Shallots (page 235), Frizzled Leeks (page 236), and Herbed Croutons (page 232) bring a stark contrast to the dishes I suggest serving them with. Moreover, each of them has its own little delicious drama going on, with a crunchy exterior giving way to a soft, silky interior. For my money, the ultimate example is Fried Oysters (page 234), which contain so much contrast that they are even compelling on their own.

As delicious as many of these are, even the best condiments and garnishes are only as good as the decision to use them; pair one with the wrong dish and it's worse than having not used any. But heed the general advice that accompanies each of the following recipes, and you'll find endless appropriate uses for them all.

Pesto

■ Makes about 1 cup ■

Pesto is an Italian basil and olive oil puree that originated in Liguria and traditionally includes Parmesan cheese, pine nuts, and garlic. It has been adapted in recent years to include everything from walnuts to parsley, but I'm a purist and only use this classic recipe.

When pesto meets heat, the big flavors of its ingredients are unlocked, so this is a wonderful thing to have in your refrigerator for a quick addition to soups or an all-you-need complement to toss with hot pasta.

1 cup pine nuts
4 cups fresh basil leaves, tightly packed
1 cup extra-virgin olive oil
½ cup freshly grated Parmesan cheese
2 cloves garlic, smashed and peeled
Coarse salt
Freshly ground black pepper

1. Put the pine nuts in a sauté pan and toast over medium-high heat, shaking them from side to side, until lightly browned and fragrant, about 3 minutes. Remove from the heat and set aside to cool completely.

2. Combine the nuts, basil, oil, Parmesan and garlic in a blender and process to a thick paste. Season with salt and pepper and blend again until smooth and creamy. If not using immediately, cover and refrigerate for up to 1 week.

Drizzle on: Tomato, Bread, and Parmesan Soup (page 40), Twice-Cooked Vegetable Soup (page 46).

Basil Oil

■ Makes about 1 cup ■

Herb oils are an easy, attractive, and unusual way to add fresh herb flavor and rich extra-virgin olive oil to a dish—with a drizzling of a colorful oil rather than simply a scattering of chopped herbs. Most herb oil recipes instruct you to strain them, but I think you get a truer flavor by leaving bits of herb in the oil.

Leaves from 1 bunch basil
    (about 1½ cups tightly packed)
1 cup extra-virgin olive oil
Coarse salt
Freshly ground black pepper

1. Bring a pot of salted water to a boil over high heat and fill a medium bowl halfway with ice water.

2. Put the basil leaves in a fine-mesh strainer, lower into the boiling water, and cook for about 5 seconds. Dip the leaves in their basket into the ice water to stop them from cooking and preserve their bright green color. Turn out the leaves onto paper towels and pat them dry.

3. Transfer the leaves to a blender, add the olive oil, and blend until the mixture turns bright green. Transfer to a bowl and let infuse for 30 to 40 minutes. Season to taste with salt and pepper. If not using immediately, cover and refrigerate for up to 3 days.

Drizzle on: Tomato, Bread, and Parmesan Soup (page 40), Twice-Cooked Vegetable Soup (page 46), Spicy Shellfish Soup (page 62).

VARIATIONS

This recipe can also be made with cilantro leaves or chives. Substitute an equal quantity of either for the basil.

Aïoli

Aïoli is a garlic mayonnaise popular in Provençal cooking as a dip for vegetables or a topping for cooked fish. I love spreading it on Croutons (pages 232 and 233) as an accompaniment to soups and stews featuring fish and shellfish.

Note: This recipe contains raw egg and should not be served to people with a compromised immune system.

3 large egg yolks
3 cloves garlic, smashed and peeled
1 cup extra-virgin olive oil
About 1 teaspoon fresh lemon juice
Pinch of cayenne pepper
Coarse salt
Freshly ground black pepper

1. Combine the egg yolks and garlic in a blender. With the machine on, add the oil gradually in a thin stream to create a thick and creamy emulsion.

2. Transfer the mixture to a bowl and stir in the lemon juice and cayenne. Taste and add more lemon juice if necessary. Season with salt and pepper. If not using immediately, cover and refrigerate for up to 2 days.

Spread on croutons and serve with: Spicy Shellfish Soup (page 62), Cod with Tomato, Saffron Broth, Leeks, and Couscous (page 148).

VARIATIONS

Red Pepper Aïoli

Reduce the quantity of garlic to 2 cloves and add 1 cup store-bought roasted pepper, rinsed and patted dry, along with the egg yolks and garlic. Spread on croutons and serve with: Mussel Chowder (page 51), Spicy Shellfish Soup (page 62).

Saffron Aïoli

Reduce the quantity of garlic to 1 clove; add 1 pinch of saffron threads (page 55) to the blender along with the egg yolks and garlic. Spread on croutons and serve with: Mussel Chowder (page 51), Mussels with Tomato and Saffron (page 54), Spicy Shellfish Soup (page 62).

Mustard Mayonnaise

Omit the garlic and add 2 tablespoons Dijon mustard along with the egg yolks.

Chopped, Roasted Tomatoes

▪ Makes 1 cup ▪

Use these tomatoes to add intense flavor to soups, stews, and other recipes.

¼ cup olive oil
Coarse salt
Freshly ground black pepper
Pinch of sugar
1 tablespoon fresh thyme leaves
12 plum tomatoes, sliced into ½-inch-thick rounds

1. Preheat the oven to 300°F.

2. Put the oil in a small bowl. Season with the oil, salt, pepper, and sugar to taste. Stir in the thyme. Dip the tomato slices in the bowl to coat them with the seasoned oil.

3. Transfer the tomatoes to a rimmed baking sheet and roast in the oven for 25 minutes until dried but not shriveled. Carefully turn them with a spatula and cook for another 5 minutes. Remove from the oven, let cool, and then chop. Refrigerate in an airtight container for up to 1 week or freeze for up to 1 month.

Herbed Croutons

If you're like me, you grew up thinking of croutons as those little pre-toasted bread squares that come in a bag or a box coated with all kinds of fake seasonings. Well, it turns out that in French cuisine they're rounds of freshly baked bread (anything from a baguette to country or peasant bread), toasted and spread with any number of toppings.

Croutons are one of my favorite ways to add crunch and flavor to a dish with little work, an almost endlessly adaptable platform for herbs, cheese, and other flavorful embellishments. In some cases, you might want to place a few croutons in the bottom of a bowl and pour soup on top; in others, you might want to serve them alongside the main event, passing them on a platter.

> **1 loaf country or peasant bread, about 1 pound,**
>   **halved lengthwise down the middle and cut into**
>   **1-inch slices**
> **About 6 tablespoons unsalted butter, at room temperature**
> **2 to 3 tablespoons chopped fresh herbs (such as thyme,**
>   **parsley, marjoram, or a combination)**
> **Coarse salt**
> **Freshly ground black pepper**

1. Preheat the broiler.

2. Lay the slices of bread on a baking sheet and spread with butter. Broil in the oven until browned, about 2 minutes, then turn, butter the other sides and brown for 2 minutes. Top each slice with some herbs and season with salt and pepper. Place under the broiler until the herbs are baked in and fragrant, about 1 minute.

3. If not serving immediately, let cool, cover and keep the croutons at room temperature for up to 2 hours. Reheat briefly on a baking sheet in a 200°F oven just before serving.

Add to: Pasta and Bean Soup (page 24), Mushroom, Barley, and Sage Soup (page 32), Mushroom Stew (page 80).

VARIATIONS

Cheese Croutons

Follow the recipe for Herbed Croutons (above), substituting 1 cup grated Gruyère or Parmesan (page 242) for the herbs.

Add to: Pasta and Bean Soup (page 24), Spinach, Parmesan, and Garlic Soup (page 34).

Garlic Croutons

▪ Makes enough to garnish 12 servings ▪

Garlic croutons are the only ones I make that bear some resemblance to those little cubed ones that come in a box. But the similarity ends with their shape. These are lightly toasted and crisped on the outside with the distinct taste of fresh garlic and a light coating of butter. I turn to these when I think the soup itself will benefit from having some crunch and garlic flavor in every bite.

4 tablespoons unsalted butter
3 tablespoons minced garlic
1 loaf peasant or country bread (about 1 pound),
   crust removed and cut into 1-inch cubes
Coarse salt
Freshly ground black pepper

1. Melt the butter in a wide, deep sauté pan over medium-high heat. Add the garlic and cook for 1 minute to soften it and infuse the butter with its flavor.

2. Add the bread to the pan and cook, tossing frequently, until the bread is crisp and golden brown, 4 to 5 minutes. Transfer to paper towels to drain. Use at once, or let cool and keep at room temperature for up to 6 hours.

Add to: Mushroom, Barley, and Sage Soup (page 32), Spinach, Parmesan, and Garlic Soup (page 34), Ham Hock and Split Pea Soup (page 66).

Fried Oysters

■ Makes 18 fried oysters, enough to garnish 6 servings ■

Fried oysters are complex and compact. Crunchy on the outside, they give way to a soft, briny interior that makes a big impact. Float them on the surface of vegetable soups or seafood chowders, or on Herbed Croutons (page 232), if necessary, to keep them dry and crisp. These are also good fun with an ice-cold beer or a vodka martini.

You will need a kitchen thermometer to keep the oil temperature constant while making this dish.

> **About 3 cups canola oil**
> **1¼ cups whole milk**
> **1 large egg**
> **18 shucked oysters, in their liquid**
> **1¼ cups all-purpose flour**
> **2½ cups dry bread crumbs or panko**
>   **(Japanese bread crumbs)**
> **Coarse salt**
> **Freshly ground black pepper**

1. Preheat the oven to 200°F. Pour the oil into a 2- or 3-quart pot to a depth of 1 inch. Heat over medium-high heat to a temperature of 350°F. Line a plate with paper towels.

2. Pour the milk into a bowl. Add the egg and whisk until well incorporated. Spread the flour out on a plate. Spread out the bread crumbs on a separate plate.

3. Remove the oysters from their liquid and pat them dry with paper towels. Dredge the oysters in the flour and, one by one, dip them in the milk. Shake them dry, then dip them in the bread crumbs.

4. Lower the oysters into the hot oil, a few at a time to avoid crowding the pot and lowering the temperature. Fry until golden brown, about 2 minutes.

5. Carefully remove the oysters with a slotted spoon and set on the paper towel-lined plate to drain. Season with salt and pepper, transfer to a baking sheet, and keep warm in the oven while you make the other oysters. (Prop the door of the oven open with a cork or folded kitchen towel to keep the heat as low as possible.) Serve as soon as all of the oysters are cooked.

Add to: Potato and Leek Soup (page 44), Extra-Smoky New England Clam Chowder (page 48).

Fried Shallots

◾ Makes enough to garnish 8 servings ◾

These small crisps look like somebody took a bowl of onion rings and accidentally shrunk them in the dryer. They taste divine, with a gentle crunch giving way to sweet shallot within. Scatter these over everything from soups to beef stews.

You will need a kitchen thermometer to keep the oil temperature constant while making this dish.

About 3 cups canola oil
3 shallots, peeled, sliced crosswise as thinly as
   possible and separated into rings
¼ cup buttermilk
⅓ cup all-purpose flour
Coarse salt
Freshly ground black pepper

1. Pour the oil into a deep pot to a depth of 1 inch. Slowly bring to a temperature of 325°F over medium-high heat. Line a plate with paper towels.

2. Meanwhile, soak the shallot rings in the buttermilk for 10 minutes. Spread the flour out on a plate and season with salt and pepper. Remove the shallots from the milk, shake off any excess liquid, dredge in the seasoned flour, then shake off any excess flour.

3. Fry the shallots in the hot oil until golden brown, about 10 seconds. Remove them with a slotted spoon and set on the paper towel-lined plate to drain. Season with salt and pepper and serve immediately.

Add to: Potato and Leek Soup (page 44), Beer and Beef Stew (page 116).

Frizzled Leeks

※　　Makes enough to garnish 8 servings　　※

When made correctly, frizzled leeks are a compelling cross between shoestring fries and the most tender onion rings you've ever tasted, a perfect adornment for any number of soups. But more often than not, they look disappointingly soggy and limp. I call these unfortunate mutants "frizzled" leeks. I've never understood why they so often come out that way, because these are actually fairly easy to make. To ensure success, remove all portions of the leek with even a trace of green color, using only the whitest, firmest part; this will allow it to maintain its shape when fried.

You will need a kitchen thermometer to keep the oil temperature constant while making this dish.

About 3 cups canola oil
2 large leeks, white part only, thick outer
    layers removed, cut crosswise into 2-inch
    sections, halved, then sliced lengthwise into
    matchstick-size strips

All-purpose flour, for dredging
Coarse salt
Freshly ground black pepper

1. Pour the oil into a deep-sided pot and heat to a temperature of 325°F over medium-high heat. Line a plate with paper towels.

2. Dredge the leeks in the flour and shake off any excess.

3. Add the leeks to the hot oil and fry until golden brown, just a few seconds. Remove with a slotted spoon and set on the paper towel-lined plate to drain. Season with salt and pepper and serve immediately.

Add to: Roasted Carrot and Ginger Soup (page 27), Potato and Leek Soup (page 44), Butternut Squash Soup with Minced Bacon (page 37, in place of the bacon).

Notes on Some Recurring Ingredients

Bacon and Other Pork Products

I'm known in culinary circles as something of a pork-o-phile, and I don't deny it. I love just about every cut of meat you can extract from the beast that no less a food authority than Homer Simpson once declared "the magical animal."

Put simply, bacon is the meat from a pig's belly, partially cooked via brine-curing and smoking. There are a number of versions, from Canadian bacon to Italian pancetta. For our purposes, I'll confine myself to those I use most often: slab bacon and double-smoked bacon, which are unsliced. Contrary to what the name suggests, double-smoked bacon isn't smoked twice; rather, it's slowly smoked to give it an even more pronounced smoky flavor than slab bacon. The flavor of double-smoked bacon differs depending upon which type of wood chips (such as apple or my favorite, hickory) is used for smoking.

I often make bacon the first ingredient to go into a pot, because it gives off a lot of fat, making it a more flavorful alternative to olive oil or butter. As for when I use which bacon, I use slab bacon in most instances and double-smoked bacon when I want an extra-smoky undercurrent.

Where can you find these? Generally speaking, any bacon kept uncut by a butcher is what you're looking for. You might also find a high-quality brand in your market's refrigerator case. Look for those that say "smoked bacon" but beware the ones that aim to trick you with the not-so-clever phrase "smoke flavored," meaning it uses liquid smoke flavoring rather than the real thing.

Double-smoked bacon may be sold in a vacuum-sealed wrapper. If it is, the outer layer of the bacon is rich with smoky flavor, though a bit tough to chew. Trim this portion and use it along with the bacon in the beginning of a recipe, then pick it out with tongs or a slotted spoon at the end of the cooking process. (Incidentally, my favorite smoked bacon is made by Schaller & Weber, see Mail-Order Sources, page 247.)

If your market doesn't have any high-quality slab bacon, you can simply revert to olive oil or butter in most cases. You can also use the omnipresent thin strips sold in your market's refrigerator case, but you won't get exactly the same flavor and they won't maintain their shape over long cooking (in fact, they'll melt away). Personally, I'd save those for breakfast and enjoy them with your eggs and toast rather than using them for cooking at other times of the day. Try thick-cut bacon instead, which will hold up better through the cooking process and is also available in most supermarkets.

Garlic Powder

No ingredient I use inspires more raised eyebrows than garlic powder, which many disdain as a poor substitute for garlic. I agree: It is a poor substitute for garlic. But I don't use it for that purpose. I use garlic powder to preseason fish and meats. It offers a more pronounced and complex flavor than the standard combination of salt and pepper.

Marjoram

I love marjoram because its flavor is utterly unique, and it gets along especially well with slow-cooked meats and braised poultry and game. I've offered substitutions for marjoram throughout the book, but if you've never tasted it, seek out fresh marjoram, especially for the way it completes the Rabbit Stew with Marjoram and Vermouth (page 130).

Parmesan Cheese (Parmigiano-Reggiano)

Ever wonder why chefs and cookbooks urge you to go to the trouble and expense of purchasing a large chunk of Parmigiano-Reggiano and grating it yourself? There are a number of good reasons, actually. First of all, though a block of imported cheese may seem expensive, you'd be surprised at the sheer volume of grated cheese just a few ounces yields. Secondly, the texture and intense flavor of freshly grated cheese is simply beyond compare. I use the small-holed side of an old-fashioned box grater for Parmesan cheese because the fine grating allows the cheese to melt more easily into a soup or pasta sauce.

Finally, Parmesan rinds are useful for flavoring simmering sauces and soups such as Tomato, Bread, and Parmesan Soup (page 40). Save rinds by tightly wrapping them in plastic wrap and starting them in the refrigerator where they will keep nearly indefinitely. They can also be frozen and thawed as needed.

Porcini Mushrooms, Dried

Even if reconstituted with water straight from the Fountain of Youth, dried porcini mushrooms will never attain the same meaty perfection they had when they were fresh. But dried porcini mushrooms are an extremely potent source of hearty mushroom flavor that can be invaluable in soups, stocks, and cooking liquids. I love it so much that I also pulverize dried porcinis into a powder (see page 123).

I skip the step of reconstituting dried porcini mushrooms in hot water before adding them to the recipes in this book because this keeps all of their flavor in the pot rather than sacrificing some of it to the soaking liquid. Just be sure to rinse them briefly under cold running water before using them, rubbing them to remove any lingering grit.

Salt, Coarse

I use coarse, Kosher salt almost exclusively. Avoid brands that contain prussiate of soda, an anti-caking agent that delays the dissolving of the salt in liquid, which makes it enormously difficult to season properly and can absolutely ruin a dish.

Stocks and Broth

As I mentioned in the Introduction, most of the recipes in this book can be made with store-bought broth. However, there are a few dishes that really benefit from homemade stocks, so if you want to make your own, here are the recipes.

Chicken Stock

5 to 6 pounds chicken bones (or chicken parts,
preferably thighs or wings, skin removed)
About 4 quarts cold water
1 large carrot, peeled and coarsely chopped
1 large onion, peeled and coarsely chopped
1 stalk celery, peeled and coarsely chopped
3 sprigs thyme
2 cloves garlic, smashed and peeled
1 tablespoon black peppercorns
2 bay leaves

1. Put the chicken bones in a large pot and add the water, making sure it covers the bones by an inch or 2, adding more water if necessary. Slowly bring to a boil over medium heat. Skim any scum that rises to the surface. Add all of the other ingredients, lower the heat, and simmer, uncovered, for at least 3 hours and up to 6 hours, until the chicken flavor is unmistakable.

2. Strain the contents of the pot through a fine-mesh strainer set over a bowl. Skim any fat that rises to the surface. Let cool, and then cover and refrigerate for up to 3 days or freeze for up to 2 months.

Vegetable Stock

About 4 quarts cold water
1 large Spanish onion, peeled and coarsely chopped
2 ribs celery, peeled and coarsely chopped
1 large leek, white part and a bit of green,
cut crosswise into large pieces, and washed well
1 plum tomato, halved and seeded

3 sprigs thyme

3 sprigs flat-leaf parsley

1 tablespoon black peppercorns

1 tablespoon coarse salt

1. Combine all of the ingredients in a stockpot, making sure the water covers the vegetables by an inch or 2, adding more water if necessary. Bring to a boil over high heat, then lower the heat and simmer, uncovered, for about 2 hours.

2. Strain the contents of the pot through a fine-mesh strainer set over a bowl. Let cool, and then cover and refrigerate for up to 3 days or freeze for up to 2 months.

Tomatoes, Fresh

To Peel Tomatoes: Bring a large pot of water to a boil. Fill a bowl with ice water and set aside. Carefully remove the stem from each tomato and cut a shallow "X" on the bottom, just deep enough to penetrate the skin. When the water boils, add the tomatoes and cook for 1 minute. Use tongs or a slotted spoon to transfer the tomatoes to the ice water. As they cool, the skins will begin to peel away. Remove the tomatoes from the water and peel.

To Seed Tomatoes: Simply cut off the top ¼ inch of the tomato, invert the fruit over a bowl or the kitchen sink, and gently squeeze until the seeds run out.

Tomatoes, Canned

Any self-respecting cook turns his or her nose up at canned fruits and vegetables, which are usually precut, far from fresh, and preserved in juices that distort their natural flavor. But there is an exception to this rule, and it's a big one. Imported, canned Italian tomatoes are a godsend, a perfectly respectable way to have great tomatoes in your kitchen year-round. My favorites are San Marzano, which isn't a brand, but refers to any tomatoes from the town of that name at the base of Mount Vesuvius, where the conditions produce superior tomatoes. If you want to make a recipe that calls for fresh tomatoes in winter, by all means turn to canned tomatoes, which I prefer to vine-ripened tomatoes, although those, too, would be fine in most cases.

One other note about tomatoes: You may have noticed that in many of my recipes, I preseason tomatoes with salt, pepper, and occasionally sugar. This is to give the tomatoes a head start, letting their natural flavor and juices combine and develop before they are introduced to the pot.

White Vinegar, Distilled

Like bacon, distilled white vinegar is one of my biggest allies in the kitchen. I use it to add a subtle but distinctly acidic lift to dishes that might otherwise seem too rich, heavy, or overwhelming. Take great care when measuring out white vinegar; if you add too much, it can backfire and turn an entire dish into something irreversibly acidic.

Mail-Order Sources

If you can't find certain ingredients in this book at your local market, you can mail-order them from these companies. This is more convenient than it might sound: Mail-ordering has never been easier than it is today. With a quick call to a toll-free number or a trip to the internet, you can have almost any specialty item delivered overnight or within a few days. I urge you to peruse these on-line specialty shops and avail yourself of their offerings.

Artisanal Cheese Center
877-797-1200
www.artisanalcheese.com
Cheeses

Browne Trading
800-944-7848
www.browne-trading.com
Fish, shellfish, caviar, and other specialties from the sea

Cook's Fresh Market
303-741-4148
www.cooksfreshmarket.com
Pork belly and other hard-to-find cuts of meat

D'Artagnan
800-327-8246
www.dartagnan.com
Duck confit, game birds, sausages, smoked and dry-cured meats, venison

Dean & Deluca
877-826-9246
www.deandeluca.com
Cheeses, olive oils, smoked fish

Kalustyan's
800-352-3451
www.kalustyans.com
Grains, chile peppers, harissa,
mustard oil, and other exotic
condiments and ingredients

Niman Ranch
www.nimanranch.com
Beef, pork, and lamb

Schaller & Weber
800-847-4115
www.schallerweber.com
Bacon, smoked bacon, and other
pork products

Urbani Truffles USA
800-327-8246
www.urbani.com
Dried porcini mushrooms

Williams-Sonoma
877-812-6235
www.williams-sonoma.com
Cookware

Acknowledgments

We had a great time taking this book from idea to reality, thanks largely to the uncommon decency, wisdom, and overall good nature of a small band of dedicated professionals. Our heartfelt gratitude to . . .

Our agent, Judith Weber, for her advice along the way;

Our editors, Beth Wareham and Rica Buxbaum Allannic. Nobody knows how to make a meeting more productive . . . or fun;

Scribner's publisher Susan Moldow, for her early support and generosity;

Scott Varricchio, Tom's assistant at Ouest, who procured our ingredients for recipe testing and kept us entertained during the process with bad jokes and good CDs;

The staff of Sobel Weber Associates, especially Anna Bliss, for their smarts and enthusiasm;

Our photographer Beatriz da Costa and her agent Mari Faucher, for their cooperative and collaborative sensibilities;

The food press of New York and the national media based here, for all of the attention and love they showed Tom during the year in which this book was written;

The staff of Ouest;

Our lovely and talented wives—what they're doing with us, we'll never know.

Index

A

aïoli, 230–31

Alison on Dominick Street, 6

ancho chile powder, 74

anchovies:

    in braised beef cheeks, 182–83

    in braised veal with tuna sauce, 194–95

    in Moroccan-spice-braised lamb

        shanks, 167–68

arborio rice, *see* risotto

artichokes, braised pork loin with, 188–89

Asian-style steamed chicken, 161

avgolemono, 42–43

B

bacon:

    baked chicken with mushrooms, pearl

        onions, and, 150–51

    in baked gnocchi carbonara, 88–89

    in beef bourguignon, 120–21

    in extra-smoky New England clam

        chowder, 48–49

    in Florentine pot roast with red wine,

        mushrooms, and tomatoes,

        178–79

    in Manhattan-style fish stew, 96–97

    minced, butternut squash soup with,

        37–38

    in mussel chowder, 51–52

    and pork products, 241–42

    in red-wine-and-tomato-braised duck,

        106–7

braised dishes (*cont.*)

    mushroom and spinach-stuffed veal breast, 197

    oxtail, with cipolline onions, 180–81

    pork belly in white wine sauce, 192–93

    pork chops in white wine sauce, 193

    pork loin with artichokes, 188–89

    pork shank, 184–85

    short ribs, mushroom-braised, 174–75

    veal shank, in white wine sauce with mushrooms, 198–200

    veal with tuna sauce, 194–95

bread:

    for croutons, 232–34

    tomato, and Parmesan soup, 40–41

    in Tuscan-style seafood stew, 60–61

    in twice-cooked vegetable soup, 46–47

brown rice, 211–12

butter:

    in butternut squash and wild mushroom risotto, 82–83

    in lamb pasticcio, 124–25

    in mashed potatoes, 221–22

    in shrimp stew with leeks, 102–3

Butterfield 81, 6

butternut squash, *see* squash

C

cabbage:

    and sausage stew, 112–13

    in twice-cooked vegetable soup, 46–47

calamari, sautéed, with white wine, garlic, and clam broth, 100–101

capellini (angel hair), 216

carbonara, baked gnocchi, 88–89

carrot, roasted, and ginger soup, 27–28

Cascabel, 6

casserole(s):

    baked gnocchi carbonara, 88–89

    lamb pasticcio, 124–25

    macaroni and goat cheese, 90–91

    spaghetti with tuna and tomato, 93

    tuna noodle, 94–95

    white bean, with preserved duck, 108–9

    white bean, with sweet sausage and sage, 109

cassoulet, 108–9

cassoulet soup, 26

cavolo nero, 47

celery salad, 145

'Cesca, 2, 6

cheese:

    in Andrew and Caitlin's soppressata lasagna, 126–27

    in baked gnocchi carbonara, 88–89

    croutons, 233

cheese: (*cont.*)

    goat, macaroni and, 90–91

    see also Parmesan cheese

chicken:

    baked, with bacon, mushrooms, and
        pearl onions, 150–51

    baked, with red wine, tomatoes,
        mushrooms, and pearl onions, 151

    braised with mushrooms, 154–55

    hearts and gizzards in Italian-style
        tomato sauce, 104–5

    in hunter-style sauce, 152–53

    lemon, and egg drop soup, 43

    in a pot, slow-cooked, 158–59

    in red wine sauce, 156–57

    and spinach soup, 35

    steamed whole, with three variations,
        160–61

    stew with marjoram and vermouth,
        131

    stock, 244

chickpea soup, 25

chili, 74–75

    Texas-style, 114–15

    venison, 128–29

chili powder, 75

chipotle peppers, 75

chowders:

    extra-smoky New England clam, 48–49

    Manhattan-style clam, 52

    mussel, 51–52

    oyster, 52

    smoked cod, 49

    see also soups

cilantro:

    mussels with ginger, scallion, and, 55

    simmered shrimp sauté with, 142

cipolline onions, 181

clam(s):

    broth, 50

    broth, sautéed calamari with white
        wine, garlic, and, 100–101

    chowder, extra-smoky New England,
        48–49

    chowder, Manhattan-style, 52

    cleaning of, 49–50

    steamed, Portuguese-style pork roast
        with, 186–87

    tubetti with white wine and, 92

cod:

    in Manhattan-style fish stew, 96–97

    with tomato, saffron broth, leeks, and
        couscous, 148–49

condiments and garnishes, 227–37

    aïoli, 230–31

    basil oil, 229

    fried oysters, 234–35

    fried shallots, 235–36

    frizzled leeks, 236–37

    garlic croutons, 233–34

    herbed or cheese croutons, 233

    pesto, 228

F

fast cooking, 8

fettuccine, 219

alla cacciatora, 153

fish, *see* seafood; *specific fish*

flank steak and pepper stew, Cuban-style, 118–19

fleur de sel, 145

Florentine pot roast with red wine, mushrooms, and tomatoes, 178–79

food processor, 22–23

France, 5

G

game birds:

mushroom-poached poussin or Cornish game hen, 166

mushroom-poached squab, 164–65

pheasant or guinea hen with bacon, mushrooms, and pearl onions, 151

garlic:

in baked chicken with bacon, mushrooms, and pearl onions, 150–51

in braised beef cheeks, 182–83

in braised pork belly in white wine sauce, 192–93

in braised pork shank, 184–85

in braised veal with tuna sauce, 194–95

in chicken braised with mushrooms, 154–55

for chicken in red wine sauce, 156–57

croutons, 233–34

gnocchi with spinach, Parmesan, and, 36

leg of lamb with, 171

in Moroccan-spice-braised lamb shanks, 167–68

in mushroom-braised short ribs, 174–75

in mussel chowder, 51–52

in potato gratin, 222–23

in rabbit stew with marjoram and vermouth, 130–31

in sausage and cabbage stew, 112–13

sautéed calamari with white wine, clam broth, and, 100–101

in slow-cooked chicken in a pot, 158–59

spinach and Parmesan soup with, 34–35

in Texas-style chili, 114–15

garlic powder, 242

ginger:

mussels with scallion, cilantro, and, 55

and roasted carrot soup, 27–28

gnocchi:

    carbonara, baked, 88–89

    with spinach, Parmesan, and garlic, 36

Gotham Bar and Grill, 5–6

grains, 207–14

green peppercorns, baked sea bass with
    tomato and, 147

grilled short rib and horseradish
    sandwich, 175

guinea hen with bacon, mushrooms, and
    pearl onions, 151

in mushroom stew, 80–81

in Portuguese-style pork roast with
    steamed clams, 186–87

in seven-hour leg of lamb, 170–71

in slow-cooked chicken in a pot,
    158–59

-stuffed veal breast, 196–97

in turkey soup with stuffing
    dumplings, 64–65

hunter-style sauce, chicken in, 152–53

H

ham hocks, 67

    and split pea soup, 66–67

harissa, for Moroccan-spice-braised lamb
    shanks, 169

herbs, assorted:

    in baked chicken with bacon,
        mushrooms, and pearl onions,
        150–51

    in braised oxtail with cipolline onions,
        180–81

    in braised pork belly in white wine
        sauce, 192–93

    for herbed croutons, 232–33

    in lobster bisque, 57–58

I

immersion blender, 22–23

introduction, 3–9

Israeli couscous, 209

Italian-style tomato sauce, chicken hearts
    and gizzards in, 104–5

K

kale, in twice-cooked vegetable soup, 46–47

kidneys, veal, with red wine and shallot,
    201–2

L

lamb:

    garlic leg of, 171

    pasticcio, 124–25

    "regular" leg of, 171

    seven-hour leg of, 170–71

    shanks, Moroccan-spice-braised,
        167–168

lasagna, Andrew and Caitlin's soppressata,
    126–27

leek(s):

    cod with tomato, saffron broth,
        couscous, and, 148–49

    in extra-smoky New England clam
        chowder, 48–49

    frizzled, 236–37

    and potato soup, 44–45

    shrimp stew with, 102

    simmered shrimp sauté with
        chanterelle mushrooms and, 142

lemon:

    baked sea bass, papillote-style, with
        olives and, 146–47

    bay scallops and tarragon risotto with,
        86

    and egg drop soups, 42–43

    shrimp and tarragon risotto with, 85–86

lentil and garlic sausage stew, 110–11

linguine, 219

    with lobster or shrimp, 59

lobster:

    bisque, 57–58

    linguine with, 59

long-grain white rice, 212–13

M

macaroni:

    and goat cheese, 90–91

    with goat cheese and roasted
        mushrooms, 91

    two-cheese, 91

    with Vermont cheddar, 91

make-ahead cooking, 8–9

Manhattan-style fish stew, 96–97

marjoram, 242

    rabbit stew with vermouth and, 130–31

mayonnaise, mustard, 231

meats, *see specific meats*

Mediterranean fish stew, 97

millet:

    basic, 209–10

    root vegetable stew with cumin,
        coriander, and, 78–79

Moroccan chicken, 161

Moroccan-spice-braised lamb shanks,
    167–68

MSG (monosodium glutamate), 14

mushroom(s):

in Andrew and Caitlin's soppressata
lasagna, 126–27

baked chicken with bacon, pearl
onions, and, 150–51

barley and sage soup with, 32–33

barley and short rib soup with, 33

in beef bourguignon, 120–21

in beef Stroganoff, 122–23

in beer and beef stew, 116–17

-braised short ribs, 174–75

chanterelle, simmered shrimp sauté
with leeks and, 142

chicken braised with, 154–55

Florentine pot roast with red wine,
tomatoes, and, 178–79

-poached poussin or Cornish game
hen, 166

-poached squab, 164–65

porcini, dried, 243

porcini powder, 123

roasted, macaroni with goat cheese
and, 91

roasting wild, 33

shiitake, simmered shrimp sauté with
scallions and, 141–42

and spinach-stuffed veal breast, 197

stew, 80–81

veal shank braised in white wine sauce
with, 198–200

wild, and butternut squash risotto,
82–84

mussel(s):

chowder, 51–52

cleaning of, 53

with ginger, scallion, and cilantro, 55

salad, 55

with tomato and saffron, 54

with white wine and scallion, 55

mustard mayonnaise, 231

N

New England clam chowder, extra-smoky,
48–49

O

olive-oil poached red snapper with
tomato and scallions, 143–44

olives, baked sea bass, papillote-style,
with lemon and, 146–47

one-pot cooking, 4–6

onion(s):

cipolline, braised oxtail with,
180–81

onion(s): (*cont.*)

in mushroom-poached squab, 164–65

pearl, baked chicken with bacon, mushrooms, and, 150–51

pearl, in beef bourguignon, 120–21

soup, sweet spring, 45

Spanish, in beer and beef stew, 116–17

Spanish, in Cuban-style flank steak and pepper stew, 118–19

Spanish, in pork medallions with barbecue sauce, 190–91

oregano, tripe with tomatoes, thyme, and, 132–34

orzo, 217

Ouest, 2, 6, 7

oxtail, braised, with cipolline onions, 180–81

oyster(s):

chowder, 52

fried, 234–35

P

papillote-style baked sea bass with lemon and olives, 146–47

pappardelle, 219

alla stracotto, 179

Parmesan cheese (Parmigiano-Reggiano), 242–43

in baked gnocchi carbonara, 88–89

gnocchi with spinach, garlic, and, 36

in lamb pasticcio, 124–25

in pasta and bean soup, 24–25

in pesto, 228

spinach and garlic soup with, 34–35

tomato and bread soup with, 40–41

in tubetti with white wine and clams, 92

in tuna noodle casserole, 94–95

in twice-cooked vegetable soup, 46–47

parsley, roasted fish and shellfish with tomatoes and, 98–99

parsnip:

roasted, and ginger soup, 29

in root vegetable stew with cumin, coriander, and millet, 78–79

pasta, 75–76, 215–20

Andrew and Caitlin's soppressata lasagna, 126–27

and bean soup, 24–25

dried, types of, 216–18

fettuccine alla cacciatora, 153

fresh, types of, 218–20

lamb pasticcio, 124–25

linguine with lobster or shrimp, 59

macaroni and goat cheese, 90–91

mushroom stew with, 81

pappardelle alla stracotto, 179

seafood, 61

red wine:

baked chicken with tomatoes, mushrooms, pearl onions, and, 151

in beef bourguignon, 120–21

in braised beef cheeks, 182–83

in braised oxtail with cipolline onions, 180–81

in classic braised beef brisket, 172–73

Florentine pot roast with mushrooms, tomatoes, and, 178–79

in mushroom stew, 80–81

sauce, chicken in, 156–57

-and-tomato-braised duck, 106–7

veal kidneys with shallot and, 201–2

ribollita, 46

rice, 211–14

brown, 211–12

in lemon and egg drop soup, 42–43

long-grain white, 212–13

wild, 213–14

risotto, 76

bay scallop, lemon, and tarragon, 86

butternut squash and wild mushroom, 82–84

leftover, in butternut squash and wild mushroom cakes, 84

leftover, in fritatta, 86

shrimp, lemon, and tarragon, 85–86

root vegetable stew with cumin, coriander, and millet, 78–79

ropa vieja, 118–19

S

saffron, 55–56

aïoli, 233

broth, cod with tomato, leeks, couscous, and, 148–49

mussels with tomato and, 54–55

in spicy shellfish soup, 62–63

sage:

mushroom, and barley soup, 32–33

white bean casserole with sweet sausage and, 109

salads:

celery, 145

leftover fish, 145

mussel, 55

salami lasagna, 127

salt, coarse, 243

sandwich(es):

beef on a string soup and, 176–77

grilled short rib and horseradish, 175

sauce(s):

barbecue, pork medallions with, 190–91

Italian-style tomato, chicken hearts and gizzards in, 104–5

for pappardelle alla stracotto, 179

tomato, for tripe with thyme and oregano, 133

tuna, braised veal with, 194–95

sauces (*cont.*)

white, with mushrooms, veal shank braised in, 198–200

white wine, braised pork belly in, 192–93

sausage:

and cabbage stew, 112–13

garlic, and lentil stew, 110–11

ground, pasticcio with, 125

sausage, sweet:

in cassoulet soup, 26

in Italian-style tomato sauce, 105

in tubetti with white wine and clams, 92

white bean casserole with sage and, 109

Savoy, Guy, 5

scallions:

mussels with white wine and, 55

olive-oil poached red snapper with tomato and, 143–44

simmered shrimp sauté with shiitake mushrooms and, 141–42

scallop(s):

lemon and tarragon risotto with, 86

stew with leeks, 103

sea bass:

baked, papillote-style with lemon and olives, 146–47

baked, with tomato and green peppercorns, 147

seafood:

Manhattan-style fish stew, 96–97

pasta, 61

roasted fish and shellfish with tomatoes and parsley, 98–99

sautéed calamari with white wine, garlic, and clam broth, 100–101

stew, Tuscan-style 60–61

see also shellfish; *specific fish*

serving food, 9

seven-hour leg of lamb, 170–71

shallots:

fried, 235–36

veal kidneys with red wine and, 201–3

shellfish:

and roasted fish with tomatoes and parsley, 98–99

soup, roasted carrot, ginger, and, 28

soup, spicy, 62–63

in Tuscan-style seafood stew, 60–61

see also seafood; *specific shellfish*

short ribs, mushroom-braised, 174–75

shrimp:

bisque, 58–59

butterflying, 87

lemon and tarragon risotto with, 85–86

linguine with lobster or, 59

sauté with chanterelle mushrooms and leeks, simmered, 142

sauté with cilantro or tarragon, simmered, 142

sauté with shiitake mushrooms and scallions, 141–42

stew with leeks, 102–3

shrimp (*cont.*)

    with white wine, garlic, and clam broth, 101

side dishes, 207–23

    barley, 207–8

    basic pasta, 215–19

    brown rice, 211–12

    butternut squash and wild mushroom risotto cakes, 84

    couscous, 208–9

    Israeli couscous, 209

    lentils, 111

    long-grain white rice, 212–13

    mashed potatoes, 221–22

    millet, 209–10

    polenta, 210–11

    potato gratin, 222–23

    ravioli, 220

    squash puree, 39

    wild rice, 213–14

slow-cooked chicken in a pot, 158–59

slow cooking, 7–8

smoked cod chowder, 49

sodium, excess of, 14

soppressata lasagna, Andrew and Caitlin's, 126–27

soups, 21–23

    beef on a string, and sandwich, 176–77

    bouillabaisse, 61

    butternut squash, with minced bacon, 37–38

cassoulet, 26

chickpea, 25

chunky corn, 31

creamy spinach, Parmesan, and garlic, 35

ham hock and split pea, 66–67

immersion blender, use of, 22–23

lemon and egg drop, 42–43

lobster bisque, 57–58

(mashed) potato and leek, 45

mushroom, barley, and sage, 32–33

mushroom, barley, and short rib, 33

mussels with tomato and saffron, 54

pasta and bean, 24–25

potato and leek, 44–45

roast carrot, ginger, and shellfish, 28

roast carrot and ginger, 27–28

roasted parsnip and ginger, 29

shrimp bisque, 58–59

silken corn puree, 30–31

spicy shellfish, 62–63

spinach, Parmesan, and garlic, 34–35

sweet, spring onion, 45

tomato, bread and Parmesan, 40–41

turkey, with stuffing dumplings, 64–65

Tuscan-style seafood stew, 60–61

twice-cooked vegetable, 46–47

see also chowders

spaghetti, 218

    with tuna and tomato, 93

spicy shellfish soup, 62–63

spinach:

    in Andrew and Caitlin's soppressata lasagna, 126–27

    and chicken soup, 35

    gnocchi with Parmesan, garlic, and, 36

    lemon and egg drop soup with, 43

    and mushroom-stuffed veal breast, 197

    Parmesan and garlic soup with, 34–35

    and white bean soup, 35

split pea soup, ham hock and, 66–67

spring onion soup, sweet, 45

squab, mushroom-poached, 164–65

squash:

    butternut, and wild mushroom risotto, 82–84

    butternut, soup with minced bacon, 37–38

    puree, 39

squid, *see* calamari

steamed dishes:

    chicken, Asian-style, 161

    chicken, tomato, 161

    Moroccan chicken, 161

    mussels with tomato and saffron, 54

    whole chicken with three variations, 160–61

stews, 77

    beef bourguignon, 120–21

    beer and beef, 116–17

    chicken hearts and gizzards in Italian-style tomato sauce, 104–5

chicken with marjoram and vermouth, 131

Cuban-style flank steak and pepper, 118–19

lentil and garlic sausage, 110–11

Manhattan-style fish, 96–97

Mediterranean fish, 97

mushroom, 80–81

rabbit, with marjoram and vermouth, 130–31

red-wine-and-tomato-braised duck, 106–7

roasted fish and shellfish with tomatoes and parsley, 98–99

root vegetable, with cumin, coriander, and millet, 78–79

sausage and cabbage, 112–13

sautéed calamari with white wine, garlic, and clam broth, 100–101

shrimp, with leeks, 102–3

tripe with tomatoes, thyme, and oregano, 132–33

tubetti with white wine and clams, 92

Tuscan-style seafood, 60–61

stock(s), 243–45

    chicken, 244

    store-bought, 14

    vegetable, 244–45

Stroganoff, beef, 122–23

T

tarragon:
    shrimp and lemon risotto with,
        85–86
    simmered shrimp sauté with, 142
Texas-style chili, 114–15
Thanksgiving leftovers, 64
thyme, tripe with tomatoes, oregano and,
    132–34
tomato(es):
    baked chicken with red wine,
        mushrooms, pearl onions, and,
        151
    baked sea bass with green peppercorns
        and, 147
    -braised duck, red-wine-and-, 106–7
    bread and Parmesan soup with, 40–41
    canned, 245–46
    for chicken in hunter-style sauce,
        152–53
    chopped roasted, 231
    in Cuban-style flank steak and pepper
        stew, 118–19
    Florentine pot roast with red wine,
        mushrooms, and, 178–79
    in mussel chowder, 51–52
    mussels with saffron and, 54–55
    olive-oil poached red snapper with
        scallions and, 143–44
    peeling and seeding fresh, 245

    in rabbit stew with marjoram and
        vermouth, 130–31
    roasted fish and shellfish with parsley
        and, 98–99
    sauce, Italian-style, chicken hearts and
        gizzards in, 104–5
    in sautéed calamari with white wine,
        garlic, and clam broth, 100–101
    spaghetti with tuna and, 93
    -steamed chicken, 161
    tripe with thyme, oregano, and, 132–34
    in Tuscan-style seafood stew, 60–61
    in venison chili, 128–129
tomorrow's table, 15
Tom Valenti's Soups, Stews, and One-Pot
    Meals, how to use, 11–15
tripe:
    with tomatoes, thyme, and oregano,
        132–33
    with white beans and tubetti, 134
tubetti, 217
    with tripe and white beans, 134
    with white wine and clams, 92
tubettini, 217
tuna:
    -noodle casserole, 94–95
    sauce, braised veal with, 194–95
    spaghetti with tomato and, 93
turkey soup with stuffing dumplings,
    64–65
Tuscan-style seafood stew, 60–61
two-cheese macaroni, 91

V

veal:

    braised, with tuna sauce, 194–95

    breast, herb-stuffed, 196–97

    breast, mushroom and spinach-stuffed, 197

    kidneys with red wine and shallot, 201–2

    shank braised in white sauce with mushrooms, 198–200

vegetable soup, twice-cooked, 46–47

vegetable stock, 244–45

venison chili, 128–29

Vermont cheddar, macaroni with, 91

vermouth, dry:

    for chicken in hunter-style sauce, 152–53

    rabbit stew with marjoram and, 130–31

    for slow-cooked chicken in a pot, 158–59

vinegar, distilled white, 246

vitello tonnato, 194–95

W

white wine:

    in baked chicken with bacon, mushrooms, and pearl onions, 150–51

    in beef Stroganoff, 122–23

    in braised pork loin with artichokes, 188–89

    in braised pork shank, 184–85

    in braised veal with tuna sauce, 194–95

    in butternut squash and wild mushroom risotto, 82–83

    in chicken braised with mushrooms, 154–55

    for chicken in hunter-style sauce, 152–53

    in cod with tomato, saffron broth, leeks, and couscous, 148–49

    in duck with dried fruits, 162–63

    in extra-smoky New England clam chowder, 48–49

    in herb-stuffed veal breast, 196–97

    in Moroccan-spice-braised lamb shanks, 167–68

    in mushroom-braised short ribs, 174–75

    in mussel chowder, 51–52

    mussels with scallion and, 55

    in rabbit stew with marjoram and vermouth, 130–31

Tom Valenti is the chef-owner of the critically acclaimed restaurant Ouest and 'Cesca, both on Manhattan's Upper West Side. He is also the cofounder of Windows of Hope, which raises funds to support the families of food-service workers who died in the World Trade Center in September 2001. When not behind the stove, he can be found fly-fishing in the river that runs through his property in East Branch, New York. He lives in New York City with his wife, Abigail, and their five cats.

Andrew Friedman, a graduate of Columbia University and The French Culinary Institute, collaborates with such prominent chefs and restaurateurs as Alfred Portale and Pino Luongo on award-winning cookbooks. This is his second collaboration with Tom Valenti. He divides his time between New York City and Chatham, New York, with his wife, Caitlin, and their trusty dog, Indy.